Retreat and Its Consequences

What are the consequences of retreat and retrenchment in foreign policy? In recent years, America has pulled back from its longtime role of international leadership. In doing so, the Obama administration has sought to conciliate adversaries; shown indifference to allies; called upon the international community to step in; proclaimed and then disavowed "red lines"; and preferred to lead from behind in the face of catastrophic civil war in Syria, ISIS barbarism in the Middle East and North Africa, Russia's predatory behavior in Eastern Europe, and China's muscle-flexing in East Asia. The consequences of this "realist" experiment have been costly and painful, and it has caused the United States to lose credibility with friends and foes. America retains the capacity to lead, but unless it resumes a more robust role, the world is likely to become a more dangerous place, with mounting threats not only to regional stability and international order, but to the country's own national interests.

Robert J. Lieber is Professor of Government and International Affairs at Georgetown University, where he has previously served as Chair of the Government Department and Interim Chair of Psychology. He is author or editor of sixteen books on international relations and US foreign policy, and he has been an adviser to presidential campaigns, to the State Department, and to the drafters of US National Intelligence Estimates.

Also by Robert J. Lieber

Author:

Power and Willpower in the American Future: Why the U.S. is Not Destined to Decline

The American Era: Power and Strategy for the 21st Century

No Common Power: Understanding International Relations

The Oil Decade: Conflict and Cooperation in the West

Oil and the Middle East War: Europe in the Energy Crisis

Contemporary Politics: Europe (co-author)

Theory and World Politics

British Politics and European Unity: Parties, Elites and Pressure Groups

Editor or Co-Editor:

Foreign Policy: Ashgate Library of Essays in International Relations

Eagle Rules? Foreign Policy and American Primacy in the 21st Century

Eagle Adrift: American Foreign Policy at the End of the Century

Eagle in a New World: American Grand Strategy in the Post-Cold War Era

Eagle Resurgent? The Reagan Era in American Foreign Policy

Eagle Defiant: U.S. Foreign Policy in the 1980s

Will Europe Fight for Oil? Energy Relations in the Atlantic Area

Eagle Entangled: U.S. Foreign Policy in a Complex World

Retreat and Its Consequences

*American Foreign Policy and
the Problem of World Order*

ROBERT J. LIEBER
Georgetown University

CAMBRIDGE
UNIVERSITY PRESS

32 Avenue of the Americas, New York, NY 10013-2473, USA

Cambridge University Press is part of the University of Cambridge.

It furthers the University's mission by disseminating knowledge in the pursuit of education, learning and research at the highest international levels of excellence.

www.cambridge.org
Information on this title: www.cambridge.org/9781107141803

© Robert J. Lieber, 2016

First published 2016

Printed in the United States of America by Sheridan Books, Inc.

A catalog record for this publication is available from the British Library

ISBN 978-1-107-14180-3 Hardback
ISBN 978-1-316-50671-4 Paperback

For Sophie, Isabel, Nate, Sydney, Lucy, and Delilah

May you live in an America with the power and purpose to fulfill its ideals at home and abroad

Contents

Figures and tables

ix

Acknowledgments

It is one of the great satisfactions of authorship to be able to thank those whose ideas, arguments, suggestions, or outright disagreements have contributed to the making of a book. In the process of conceiving this work and carrying it through to completion, I have gained from frequent exchanges with academic and professional colleagues. Some (I hope many) will agree with the conclusions I have drawn, others will share some but not all of the argument, and at least a few will strenuously disagree. It is thus a pleasure to acknowledge those from whose ideas or arguments I have benefitted. They include Amatzia Baram, Robert Burkett, Benjamin J. Cohen, Eliot Cohen, Josep Colomer, Sally Cowal, Mick Cox, Donald Downs, Edward Friedman, Louis Goodman, Ariya Hagh, Jeffrey Herf, Dan Hopkins, Arie M. Kacowicz, Matthew Kroenig, Mark Lagon, Christopher Layne, Keir Lieber, Nancy Lieber, Charles Lipson, Sean Long, Tim Lynch, Michael Mandelbaum, Evan B. Montgomery, Henry Nau, Dani Nedal, T.V. Paul, Jon Pevehouse, Allis and Ronald Radosh, Gil Rozman, Catherine Sandstrom, Dan Schueftan, Avraham Sela, Ruth Weisberg, and two anonymous manuscript reviewers for Cambridge University Press. In addition, I especially appreciate the valuable comments and research assistance of Michael Stecher as well as his and Sean Long's help in preparing the tables of GDP data.

Throughout the writing process I have gained from discussions in conferences, lectures, seminars, debates, and through informal conversations. In an increasingly polarized and sometimes dysfunctional academic world, the ability nonetheless to maintain civil discourse about ideas is not to be taken for granted. I have benefitted from the opportunity to present my ideas in venues at home and abroad. In addition to Georgetown, these have included George Washington University, Johns Hopkins University, Marquette University, University of Southern California, University of Tokyo, University of Wisconsin, Annual Meetings of the American Political Science Association, and policy conferences in Lisbon and Prague.

In developing the argument of this book, I have drawn in part on insights and ideas from my previous work. Where I have directly used material, I have footnoted this with specific reference to the prior writing. Emphasis on the importance of America's role in sustaining world order can be found in my two most recent books, *The American Era: Power and Strategy for the 21st Century* (Cambridge University Press, 2007), and *Power and Willpower in the American Future: Why the United States is Not Destined to Decline* (Cambridge University Press, 2012). Chapter 3 is based in part on a paper, "Rhetoric or Reality? American Grand Strategy and the Contemporary Middle East," delivered at the Annual Meeting of the American Political Science Association, Washington DC, August 28–31, 2014. Chapter 4 revises and updates my article, "The Rise of the BRICS and American Primacy," *International Politics* (London), Vol. 51, No. 2 (March, 2014): 137–154, and is reprinted with the permission of Palgrave Macmillan Journals.

In addition, I am grateful for institutional and research support from Georgetown University, especially a sabbatical from the Government Department and College of Arts and Sciences, and a senior faculty fellowship from the Graduate School. Finally it is a special pleasure to thank Lewis Bateman, senior editor at Cambridge University Press for his sage advice and support. His knowledge, wisdom, and judgment are all too rare in today's publishing world.

Introduction

Is the active engagement and leadership of a powerful America essential for its own security and the maintenance of world order? In recent years, that long-standing logic of American foreign policy has been called into question and we have been witnessing a change in foreign policy as America has gradually but unmistakably been pulling back from its customary international role. But does a foreign policy strategy of retrenchment and selective disengagement enhance or threaten America's own national interests and the stability of global order?

In seeking to answer these questions, this work builds in part upon my two latest books. In *The American Era: Power and Strategy for the 21st Century* (Cambridge University Press, 2005 and 2007), I argued that external threats, the weakness of international institutions in confronting global dangers, and the unique strength and power of the United States combined to make a grand strategy of active engagement a necessary adaptation to the realities of the post-9/11 world. This orientation seemed vital not only for the benefit of America's own national security but also for the stability of the international order.

That book and intensified debates about the effects and legitimacy of American foreign policy led to a subsequent project in which I asked the question of whether the United States still possessed the capacity to continue this distinctive role or if changes occurring both abroad and at home meant that it could or should no longer do so. In that work, *Power and Willpower in the American Future: Why the United States is Not Destined to Decline* (Cambridge University Press, 2012), I concluded that America's material strengths remained substantial, but a series of policy problems, institutional limits, normative questions, and political polarization had become more central in shaping and constraining the role of the United States.

That background, together with increasing and largely unpredicted crises in the Middle East (ISIS, Iraq, Syria, Libya, and Yemen), Eastern Europe

Aim of Book

(Russia's breach of the post-1945 European order) and elsewhere leads me to the new work. In this, I examine the implications of a reduced US role. This pattern of foreign policy retrenchment is a consequence of choices made by the administration of President Barack Obama, in the context of events that have occurred in the past decade and a half. The retrenchment process is uneven and more subtle in some areas and functions than in others. It has been driven by presidential predilections, but also by public disillusion with the results of long wars in Afghanistan and Iraq, as well as by complex policy dilemmas, the intractability of regional problems, economic and budgetary constraints, and the rise of China and other regional powers. And it has been rationalized and applauded by "realists" from both the academic and policy worlds.

Drive by

America's pullback has been undertaken in the belief that doing so would reduce conflict, encourage the international community to "step up" in assuming the burdens of regional stability, protect America's own national interests, and promote global order.[1] Yet the actual results of this policy suggest that the opposite may be the case. Disorder has many causes, but we now face a far more dangerous and disorderly world with the rise of hostile powers, fanatical terrorist movements, and worsening regional conflicts in Europe, the Middle East, and Asia. Meanwhile, our allies are in disarray and our senior military and intelligence leaders warn of increasing threats to America itself.

Aim policy

But

These events bring us back to the question of whether in the world as it is today a robust American role is a prerequisite for regional and global order and for its own safety and prosperity. In the mid-to-late 1990s, at a time when US primacy seemed unchallenged in the aftermath of the Cold War and collapse of the Soviet Union, America was for a time described as "indispensable."[2] In the following years, the phrase came to be praised, criticized, and by some even ridiculed. Nonetheless, the experiences of recent years provide compelling evidence about the adverse consequences of retrenchment. Though active engagement by the United States cannot be a sufficient condition for world order, the evidence suggests it is a necessary one.

??

---

[1] Signposts for this evolution in US policy can be found in President Obama's policy speeches. See especially, the Cairo speech, *New York Times*, June 4, 2009; the Nobel Prize acceptance address, December 10, 2009, www.nobelprize.org/nobel_prizes/peace/laureates/2009/obama-lecture_ en.html; a US Military Academy speech on Afghanistan policy, December 1, 2011, www.whitehouse .gov/the-press-office/remarks-president-address-nation-way-forward-afghanistan-and-pakistan; the Fort Bragg speech on the end of the Iraq War, December 14, 2011, www.whitehouse.gov/ the-press-office/2011/12/14/remarks-president-and-first-lady-end-war-iraq; a foreign policy speech to West Point graduates, May 28, 2014, www.whitehouse.gov/photos-and-video/video/2014/05/28/ president-obama-speaks-west-point-graduates; and the American University address on the Iran nuclear agreement, August 5, 2015, www.washingtonpost.com/news/post-politics/wp/2015/08/05/ text-obama-gives-a-speech-about-the-iran-nuclear-deal/.

[2] One of the earliest uses of the term occurs in Bill Clinton's second inaugural address. In his words, "America stands alone as the world's indispensable nation." January 20, 1997, www .bartleby.com/124/pres65.html.

In the chapters that follow, I develop these arguments. Chapter 1, "Foreign policy retreat and the problem of world order," examines how in the last half of the twentieth century and the early years of the twenty-first, the United States was the strongest power and the leading actor in world affairs. In recent years, however, America's status and role have undergone a pronounced change. Globalization has fostered the diffusion of power, and with the dramatic rise of China and the emerging importance of regional actors, American predominance is no longer self-evident. Meanwhile, the human and material costs of a decade of grinding warfare in Afghanistan and Iraq and the impact of the great financial crisis of 2008–9 have left many Americans wary of spending blood and treasure abroad. Added to these factors, many foreign policy experts, especially realist scholars, and some leading political figures have called for America to adopt a foreign policy of restraint and retrenchment, acting as an offshore balancer, and pulling back from foreign and security policy commitments in Europe, the Middle East, and Asia. The foreign policy of the Obama administration has exemplified this trend, albeit in a nuanced way, and the president himself made ending the Iraq and Afghan wars the leitmotif of his administration. However, based on the experience of recent years, there is compelling evidence that protecting the country's own security as well as sustaining the rules and institutions of post-1945 and post–Cold War order requires enhanced American engagement.

Chapter 2, "Burden sharing with Europe: problems of capability and will," examines the deep changes that have taken place within Europe and in its relationship with the United States. For much of the past half-century, Europe together with Japan and the United States had been a pillar of the international order, but it now lags in its capacity to play that role. International rules, norms, and institutions that are so widely embraced as an alternative to the old geopolitics and the great conflicts of the twentieth century require active American participation and European engagement to sustain them. But in circumstances where the United States has downplayed its European engagements and Europeans themselves have become less capable and more inclined to hedge their bets, the future of the Atlantic partnership and of long-established international institutions and regimes is far from assured.

Chapter 3, "Middle East policy: regional conflicts and threats to national interests" assesses the shifts in US Middle East policy that have emerged in recent years. Rather than provide an effective basis for policy and strategy, the consequences of this approach have been counterproductive. US national interests in the region have long included security of oil supplies, preventing territorial control by hostile powers, support of regional friends and allies, maintenance of regional stability, counterterrorism, nuclear nonproliferation, and – at least rhetorically – democracy and human rights. These provide a benchmark for comparisons of policy effects over time. Though the Bush administration's 2003 invasion of Iraq and its removal of Saddam Hussein's tyrannical regime led to a power vacuum and years of upheaval and lethal conflict there, the combination of the United States-led surge and the role of the Sunni tribes in the "awakening" movement had by 2009 restored a greater degree of order and a tenuous peace among Sunnis, Shiites, and Kurds. Subsequently, the December 2011 withdrawal of US forces greatly reduced American influence over the Maliki regime and forfeited the precarious stability that had been achieved at such high cost. More broadly within the region, a slow but perceptible trend of American retrenchment has contributed to a more dangerous and unstable Middle East. Elsewhere, a pattern of conciliatory policies toward Iran and Russia has had spillover effects on traditional allies. This regional case and its wider implications lend support to the broader argument about the importance of American engagement for sustaining global order and the adverse consequences of a diminished role.

Chapter 4, "BRICS: stakeholders or free-riders?" asks whether rising regional powers (Brazil, Russia, India, China, South Africa, and others) can or will play a greater role in sustaining global order at a time when the relative weight of Europe and Japan has appeared to recede. Some scholars and political observers foresee the BRICS countries not only becoming more influential in world affairs, but also reshaping and promoting international institutions and regimes in an increasingly multipolar world. However, in reality, the BRICS have been less rather than more cooperative in maintaining or enhancing the existing global order. Consequently, a combination of American retrenchment and BRICS abdication tends to weaken not only multilateral institutions but the wider international order itself.

Chapter 5, "Retreat and its consequences," considers the case for retrenchment and then surveys the results in foreign and domestic policy. For more than seven decades, America has supported global order and served as the leader, defender, and promoter of the liberal democracies and market economies. This brings us back to long-standing arguments about the importance of a liberal great power to provide the hegemonic stability necessary for the successful functioning of an open, prosperous international economic order – a role played by Britain in the nineteenth century and until 1914, and after World War II by the United States.[3] Others, however, are more complacent about the stability of the international order. Liberal internationalists have claimed that institutions and international regimes already constitute a quasi-constitutional order or that these organizations and regimes can be self-sustaining and even created in the absence of a hegemonic leader. Academic realists are still more skeptical about the need and desirability of US leadership, asserting that without the United States, regional actors will balance against threats, but that in the unlikely event its own security interests are endangered, America has the capacity to reengage as needed. The evidence, especially in response to the most

---

[3] The seminal works are those of Charles Kindleberger, *The World in Depression: 1929–1939*, (Berkeley: University of California Press, 1973); and Robert Gilpin, *War and Change in World Politics* (New York: Cambridge University Press, 1981).

urgent and deadly crises, suggests otherwise, as in the inadequacy or outright failure of international institutions and regional powers in cases such as those of Ukraine, Syria, Libya, Rwanda, Bosnia, North Korea, and the Congo. In short, to the question of whether the United States remains indispensable for collective action on common world problems, the answer is yes.

Finally, Chapter 6, "Can America still lead – and should it?" makes the case that America's capacity to lead remains only marginally diminished and that by almost all the criteria by which power is measured it retains a unique position. To be sure, there are material constraints: entitlement programs urgently need changes so that their costs do not create unsustainable problems of debt and deficit, immigration policy requires wholesale reform, and major infrastructure needs must be dealt with. In addition, in the absence of policy change, scheduled reductions in defense spending, troop levels, and weapons will shrink the military's share of GDP to the lowest level since Pearl Harbor and endanger its capacity to meet major threats. Moreover, political polarization poses a problem in itself. Congress remains more deeply divided than at any time since the end of reconstruction in the late 1870s,[4] and the effectiveness of governmental institutions is far from ideal.

Yet if the United States retains the capacity to lead, the will to do so is much less certain, as are judgments about where and how. Arguments for retrenchment have become increasingly prominent in both the policy realm and in the academic literature of international relations. Upon taking office, President Obama was by no means alone in his call for refocusing on "nation-building at home" and, at the time, the public had become increasingly skeptical about America's world role. However, in response to growing threats including the rise of ISIS and concerns about terrorism, recent polls do show an increase in the percentage of Americans willing to support more forceful policies, though considerable reluctance persists. Ultimately however, and despite pressing domestic problems, the United States will eventually need to resume a more robust role, whether due to deliberate changes in policy or to the pressure of unforeseen events. America retains the capacity to lead, but unless it does so, the world is likely to become a more disorderly and dangerous place, with mounting threats not only to world order and economic prosperity, but to its own national interests and homeland security.

---

[4] Nolan McCarty, Keith T. Poole, and Howard Rosenthal, *Polarized America: The Dance of Ideology and Unequal Riches* (Cambridge, MA: MIT Press, 2006); and "The Polarization of the Congressional Parties," updated January 19, 2014, http://polarizedamerica.com/political_polarization.asp.

Foreign policy retreat and the problem of world order

> Looking back over my more than half a century in intelligence, I have not experienced a time when we have been beset by more crises and threats around the globe.
>
> – James R. Clapper, Director of National Intelligence[1]

During the last half of the twentieth century and the early years of the twenty-first, the United States was the preeminent power and leading actor in world affairs. This role took many forms: allied leader of the Big Three powers in World War II, creator and sustainer of international institutions and the postwar international order, head of the Western alliance during the Cold War, and lone superpower in the post–Cold War era. In those years, America supported regional stability, provided deterrence and reassurance for allies, led efforts at nonproliferation, underwrote much of the world economy, fostered trade liberalization, and often (though not always) encouraged human rights and democratization. In doing so, it served, in effect, as the world's leading provider of public goods.

In recent years, however, America's status and role have undergone a pronounced change. In the years after the 9/11 terrorist attacks on New York and Washington, the United States experienced long and costly wars in Iraq and Afghanistan, the 2008–9 global financial crisis, and the Great Recession. The international arena has also changed. Foreign policy now takes place in an increasingly globalized world in which power has become much more diffused than was the case during the Cold War (1945–91) and in the initial decade of the post–Cold War era. Simultaneously, the BRICS (Brazil, Russia, India,

[1] Remarks as delivered by James R. Clapper, Director of National Intelligence, Worldwide Threat Assessment to the Senate Select Committee on Intelligence, January 29, 2014, Washington, DC, http://icontherecord.tumblr.com/post/74958293225/remarks-as-delivered-by-james-r-clapper-director.

China, and South Africa) and others have seemingly emerged as significant actors in world affairs. The appearance of these and other rising powers is not entirely new, but together they represent an increased presence in economic, cultural, political, and even security terms, and some authors describe their rise as altering the international balance of power, marking an end to the postwar American order.[2]

At the same time, the relative influence of America's longtime allies, Europe and Japan, has ebbed as these traditional centers of power have seen economic and demographic stagnation and increasing political disarray. Within the European Union (EU), both expanding to twenty-eight countries and deepening in the functions it now encompasses, have fostered greater internal divisiveness over the burdens and costs of membership, the extent to which governance of key functions should be shifted to Brussels, and intrusions on national sovereignty. Policy disagreements have also intensified, especially over economic strategies, energy, a massive surge of Middle East refugees, and the degree to which Russia should be confronted over its aggressive actions in Ukraine and Eastern Europe.

A serious rift over Greece and the Eurozone exemplifies many of these tensions. After an initial burst of optimism and apparent success when the Euro was created in 1999 and became an actual common currency in 2002, its now nineteen member countries have in recent years found themselves in an increasingly difficult crisis. Creation of a currency union but not an accompanying economic or political union left Eurozone member countries without the flexibility to adapt in the face of differences in growth rates, competitiveness, and indebtedness. A dispute over Greece's unmanageable debt left EU countries deeply divided over policy and Europe's future. At the same time, Britain, a pillar of the international order and longtime partner of America, has seen a rise in anti-EU sentiment and faces a referendum on the possibility of withdrawal. The United Kingdom also risks fragmentation if Scotland were to secede. In addition, as a result of steep cuts in the military, its capacity to project power abroad has been greatly diminished.

Europe's economic and demographic indicators have also become unfavorable. Gross Domestic Product (GDP) in the Eurozone countries as well as in Japan has yet to regain the pre-financial crisis peak of early 2007.[3] And with the exception of France and Britain, long-term birth rates for almost all of

---

[2] For example, Jonathan Kirshner, *American Power after the Financial Crisis* (Ithaca, NY: Cornell University Press, 2014). He argues that the impact of the global economic crisis that began in 2008 undermined the legitimacy of the economic ideas underpinning the American led order, and he sees its consequence as the erosion of US power and the increased influence of China and other rising powers.

[3] US real GDP, seven years after the pre-crisis peak in Q4, 2007, had increased 8.1 percent, but in the Eurozone, since Q1, 2008, GDP remained down by 2.2 percent and in Japan down by 1.1 percent. See *Outlook: U.S. Preeminence*, Investment Management Division, Goldman Sachs, January 2015, Exhibit 4, p. 8.

these countries remain far below the level required for population replenishment. Indeed, no less a figure than Pope Francis, in an address to the European Parliament in Strasbourg, cautioned that the world now views Europe as "somewhat elderly and haggard."[4]

Meanwhile, global disorder has been growing. Military threats to international order come from revisionist states, especially Russia, Iran, and China, as well as from non-state and quasi-state actors, mainly al-Qaeda, ISIS, and Hezbollah. The actions of Russia under President Putin blatantly violate not only the post 1945 European order, but the rules, understandings, and treaties underpinning the global order and contemporary international law since the end of World War II. In breaching national borders by force and in its multiple intrusions on the state sovereignty of its neighbors, Moscow contravenes the principles of the UN Charter, the Helsinki Declaration of 1975, the Budapest Memorandum of 1994 (guaranteeing the sovereignty of Ukraine), and the NATO–Russia Founding Act of 1997. Russia also has violated the rules of the Intermediate Nuclear Forces Treaty (INF) of 1987, the Conventional Forces in Europe (CFE) treaty of 1990, and other formal agreements.

Russia is not the only major power challenger. China has been flexing its muscles in the East and South China Seas, where it has asserted sovereignty over wide areas that encroach on territorial waters of its Asian neighbors. In doing so it has acted aggressively with the increased presence of its air and naval forces. At the same time, Beijing has been steadily expanding its military capacity to deter or even to defeat US forces that are supposed to support and defend regional allies.

Iran, though not a great power, has emerged as the most dangerous state actor in the Gulf and Levant. By means of Shiite militias and clients, it exercises major influence over important regional capitals: Baghdad, Damascus, Beirut, and Sana (Yemen). As a result of the July 2015 Vienna nuclear agreement, the Joint Comprehensive Plan of Action (JCPOA), Iran will after five years be free of restrictions on weapons imports and in eight years be without hindrance to its continuing development of intercontinental ballistic missiles. These missiles only make sense militarily if fitted with nuclear warheads, and they will have the range to reach Israel, Europe, and ultimately the United States. And even if Iran fully complies with the terms of the JCPOA, it will after fifteen years emerge with modern nuclear facilities and enrichment capacity and by that time, according to even the most optimistic projections, be no more than one year from the achievement of a nuclear weapons capability. Should Iran do so, this is likely to lead to a multinuclear Middle East and the collapse of the nonproliferation regime. Moreover, Iran's longtime use of terrorism through proxies such as Hezbollah remains part of its foreign policy toolbox not only in the region, as in Lebanon, Syria, Iraq,

4 "Pope Francis Complains of 'haggard' Europe in Strasbourg," BBC News Europe, November 25, 2014, www.bbc.com/news/world-europe-30118066.

Yemen, Bahrain, and Gaza, but in places as widespread as Argentina, Bulgaria, and Thailand.[5]

As for non-state and quasi-state threats to global order, the Islamic State/ISIS and al-Qaeda (both of which are Sunni), and Shiite Hezbollah along with Shiite militias backed by Iran, though sometimes in deadly conflict with each other, pose growing threats in the Levant and more widely in North Africa, the Sahel, Nigeria, Kenya, Somalia, and elsewhere. Volunteers pouring into the ranks of ISIS come not only from the Middle East and Asia, but from disaffected young men (and some women) living in Europe and to a much lesser extent the United States. Those with Western passports who survive their involvements with radical Islamist militant groups pose a very real threat as they return home. The November 2015 attack killing 130 people in Paris provided graphic evidence of that threat.

Global and regional threats and disorder are not only evident in terms of military security and terrorism. Since 9/11, and increasingly in recent years, there has been marked erosion in human rights and a rise in authoritarianism. During this period, and in contrast to the promise of the post–Cold War decade, some twenty-five countries have witnessed the severe erosion or breakdown of democracy, including such prominent cases as Turkey, Russia, Thailand, Kenya, Venezuela, Bangladesh, and Ecuador.[6]

RETRENCHMENT IN POLICY AND THEORY

In this changing and in many ways more threatening geopolitical environment, arguments for retrenchment have become increasingly prominent in both the policy realm and in the academic literature of international relations. Proponents have argued that America should pull back from extensive foreign engagements for reasons of reduced capability and the absence of vital national interest and that its security and interests can be protected by remaining an offshore balancer. This preference for retrenchment in foreign policy is reinforced by a combination of policymaker beliefs, domestic economic and political constraints, and by public disillusionment with the experiences of intervention. → Why it has gained support   *e.g.*
Obama

President Obama's approach to foreign policy reflected a clear preference for reducing US power and presence abroad, a deep skepticism about the use of force, an emphasis on working in and through international institutions, an "extended hand" to adversaries in the expectation that this could incentivize significant changes in their behavior, a de-emphasis on relationships with allies, and a desire to focus on domestic priorities.

---

[5] For example, Iran's Hezbollah proxy was responsible for terrorist attacks in Argentina in 1992 and 1994 and in Bulgaria in 2012.

[6] Larry Diamond, "Facing Up to the Democratic Recession," *Journal of Democracy*, Vol. 26, No. 1 (January 2015), pp. 141–155, www.journalofdemocracy.org/article/facing-democratic-recession.

[handwritten: Evidence of retrenchment under Obama.]

As a consequence, recent years have seen a shift from previous American policy and practice and a reduced degree of global engagement. Obama emphasized ending the wars in Afghanistan and Iraq, decided against military assistance to moderate rebels in the early years of the Syrian civil war, did little to support stabilization in Libya after the overthrow of Gaddafi, reached out to the Russians with a policy "reset," overruled his senior foreign policy advisers in refusing to provide effective defensive weapons to Ukraine in the initial phase of Russia's intervention, offered an extended hand to the Islamic Republic of Iran, and presided over major cuts in the defense budget and US troop strength. Despite increasing security challenges and regional disorder, the Obama 2015 National Security Strategy stressed "strategic patience," signaling a continuing preference for distancing.[7]

Foreign policy realist scholars have intensified or repeated arguments that many of them have been making since the end of the Cold War, in calling for a shift to offshore balancing and disengagement from commitments in the Middle East, Asia, and Europe.[8] Realists largely oppose the positioning of substantial military bases and forces abroad. For some, this change is necessary in order to devote resources to priorities at home and rekindle economic growth or because they believe America can no longer afford costly interventions abroad.[9] Others emphasize avoiding foreign entanglements and see offshore balancing as the preferred foreign policy strategy. They believe that in the absence of the United States, balance of power logic will cause regional powers to balance against threats in Europe, the Persian Gulf, Northeast Asia, and elsewhere. As a result, America need not expend its own resources of blood and treasure in doing so.[10] In the meantime, thanks to geographic distance and the buffer provided by two large oceans, we can avoid entanglement in most foreign conflicts. And if it does become necessary for the United States to intervene, it should utilize its natural advantages in air and naval strength rather than employ large land forces.[11] In practice, however, the concept

[handwritten: limit American deaths]

[7] *National Security Strategy*, The White House, Washington DC, February 2015, www.whitehouse.gov/sites/default/files/docs/2015_national_security_strategy_2.pdf.

[8] For an elaboration of realist arguments for retrenchment, see Chapter 5.

[9] Daniel Drezner, "Military Primacy Doesn't Pay (Nearly As Much As You Think)," *International Security*, Vol. 38, No. 1 (Summer 2013), pp. 52–79; Christopher Layne, "This Time It's Real: The End of Unipolarity and the 'Pax Americana,'" *International Studies Quarterly* (February 2012), pp. 1–11.

[10] For example, Eric Nordlinger, *Isolationism Reconfigured: American Foreign Policy for a New Century* (Princeton, NJ: Princeton University Press, 1995); Joseph M. Parent and Paul K. MacDonald, "The Wisdom of Retrenchment: America Must Cut Back to Move Forward," *Foreign Affairs*, Vol. 90, No. 6 (November/December, 2011), pp. 32–47; Stephen M. Walt, "Offshore Balancing: An Idea Whose Time Has Come," *Foreignpolicy.com*, November 2, 2011, http://foreignpolicy.com/2011/11/02/offshore-balancing-an-idea-whose-time-has-come/.

[11] See, for example, Christopher Layne, "From Preponderance to Offshore Balancing," *International Security*, Vol. 22, No. 1 (Summer 1997), pp. 86–124; and John Mearsheimer, "Imperial by Design," *The National Interest*, No. 111 (January/February 2011), pp. 16–24 at p. 16.

provides a rationale for inaction and as critics have noted, offshore balancing is much more attractive as an academic notion than a real-world strategic approach.[12]

A leading realist thinker, Barry R. Posen, argues that America can safely pull back from many of its overseas commitments, and in an earlier work he posits that "command of the commons" – that is, dominance in air, sea, and space – provides the latitude for the United States to play this more distant role.[13] Joshua Rovner contends that the Obama administration has done some things very well, "blending activism and restraint in order to deal with present threats without getting mired in unsolvable long-term quagmires."[14] Other realist scholars argue that the United States has no national security interest in Syria and that it should avoid entanglement in Ukraine, which some see as a legitimate Russian sphere of interest in which Kiev's desire for an agreement with the EU and its (unrequited) aspirations for a NATO connection have provoked Moscow.[15] At times, realist proponents have appeared hyperbolic, as in John Mearsheimer's claim that, "From neoconservatives on the right to liberal imperialists on the left, there has been no meaningful diminishment in their commitment to intervening in countries all across the globe."[16]

What realist thinkers also have in common is a reductive view of foreign policy behavior that undervalues the ideology, beliefs, and interests of foreign actors and regimes. Indeed, even Kenneth Waltz, whose seminal work over the past half-century defined structural realism, had warned against too deterministic a use of its concept. In his words:

Structures shape and shove. They do not determine behaviors and outcomes, not only because unit-level and structural causes interact, but also because the shaping and shoving of structures may be successfully resisted.[17]

---

[12] Bryan McGrath and Ryan Evans, "American Strategy and Offshore Balancing by Default," *War on the Rocks*, August 27, 2013, http://warontherocks.com/2013/08/the-balance-is-not-in-our-favor-american-strategy-and-offshore-balancing-by-default.

[13] Barry R. Posen, "Command of the Commons: The Military Foundation of U.S. Hegemony," *International Security*, Vol. 28, N. 1 (summer 2003), pp. 5–46; *Restraint: A New Foundation for U.S. Grand Strategy* (Ithaca, NY: Cornell University Press, 2014); and "Just Say No: America Should Avoid These Wars," *The National Interest*, February 10, 2015, http://nationalinterest.org/feature/just-say-no-america-should-avoid-these-wars-12217#.

[14] Joshua Rovner, "Hidden Victories," *Lawfare*, February 8, 2015, www.lawfareblog.com/2015/02/the-foreign-policy-essay-hidden-victories/.

[15] For example, Stephen Walt, "Why Arming Kiev Is a Really, Really Bad Idea," *Foreign Policy*, February 9, 2015, http://foreignpolicy.com/2015/02/09/how-not-to-save-ukraine-arming-kiev-is-a-bad-idea/?utm_source=Sailthru&utm_medium=email&utm_term=*Morning%20Brief&utm_campaign=2014_MorningBrief%2002%2010%2015%20.

[16] John J. Mearsheimer, "America Unhinged," *National Interest*, January–February 2014.

[17] Kenneth Waltz, "Reflections on Theory of International Politics: A Response to My Critics," in Robert O. Keohane, ed., *Neorealism and Its Critics* (New York, Columbia University Press, 1986), p. 343.

This caution is useful. The international distribution of power and the relative strength of a country create propensities for certain types of behavior, but do not by themselves determine behavior. Thus, whatever the external incentives to behave as normal powers, the conduct of Russia, China, Iran, and others is deeply influenced by internal factors, especially their histories, ideologies, and sense of national grievances. Realists tend to assume that countries will act based mainly upon their own capabilities and the international distribution of power and that these sources of conduct outweigh internal factors in shaping state behavior. For example, during the Cold War, Waltz argued that there were parallelisms between the policies of the United States and the USSR, both of them acting as superpowers and making decisions that gave more weight to their geopolitical power interests than to the values and ideologies that divided them.

In a related way, President Obama's conciliatory approach is consistent with realist beliefs that downplay the internal motivations of states. His outreach to adversaries, offer of the extended hand, and reluctance to counter the actions of Russia, China, and Iran assumes that their conduct is shaped in substantial measure or even primarily in reaction to American rhetoric and policy. The evidence for that proposition is slim, yet both realist logic and the Obama approach downplay the agency of other states, that is, the autonomous identity and motivation that shapes their actions and conduct. For Obama, one element of this has been the belief that globalization, trade, and information technology will gradually reshape behavior. The Obama opening to Cuba exhibited this logic, as did his observations about Iran, including his remarks that if "their economy becomes more integrated with the world economy, then in many ways it makes it harder for them to engage in behaviors that are contrary to international norms."[18] → Obama's logic

The recent history of Russian and Chinese behavior casts doubt on such assumptions. In the case of Russia, despite a post–Cold War quarter-century of extensive exposure and engagement with the West and greatly expanded trade, travel, and communications, President Putin has imbued his country with an increasingly radical nationalism and revanchism, subverting and annexing Crimea, invading Ukraine, threatening Poland and the Baltic countries, and consolidating a thuggish autocracy at home. The case of China is at least as striking. Since its economic opening in 1978 under Deng Xiaoping, and despite an unprecedented degree of globalization and trade, decades of spectacular economic growth, and a vast increase in interdependence, China's Communist leaders in recent years have adopted confrontational policies toward their neighbors and the United States and in recent years have tightened their authoritarian control.

As further evidence for the importance of internal sources of state conduct, social scientist Gilbert Rozman provides a rigorous analysis of Russian and Chinese conduct. Rozman identifies six broad factors shaping their national

---

[18] Quoted in Jackson Diehl, "Obama Rolls the Dice on Iran," *Washington Post*, April 13, 2015.

identity in opposition to Western concepts of world order.[19] First, both①
Russia and China justify their rule by taking pride in the erstwhile socialist era
and seek to project their existing political order outward and in opposition to
"anti-hegemonism" (shorthand for American influence.) Second, they stress past②
historical differences with the West and especially the Cold War with the United
States. Third, Moscow and Beijing depict the 2008–9 financial crisis as signaling③
the failure of the Western economic and political model, and both have recently
increased their repression of civil society more than at any time in the past two
decades. Fourth, Presidents Putin and Xi Jinping have prioritized bilateral rela-④
tions between their two countries. This results from their mutual emphasis on
the importance of the Communist legacy. In China, this remains the prevailing
ideology, and in Russia it is treated as largely positive historical inheritance. In
consequence, they attract few natural allies. Fifth, they prioritize international⑤
political cooperation with each other, minimizing their differences and exaggerat-
ing threats from America and its allies. And sixth, both Putin and Xi have strongly⑥
emphasized national identity and themes of historic grievance, and both have
adopted shrill propaganda and chauvinistic rhetoric to justify domestic repression and confrontational foreign policies. These policies tend to resonate domesti-
cally because of the real or imagined national memories they evoke. And for both
Russia and China, this has resulted in more strident nationalism than at any time
since the Cold War.

This analysis offers an effective counter to arguments that Western actions in
expanding NATO and in support of Ukraine's quest for economic and political
liberalization and closer ties to the EU have provoked Moscow's belligerence.[20]
It also suggests analogies with Cuba and Iran. In the case of Cuba, the
Communist party retains tight control of the state machinery including the
security services, military, judiciary, economy, and the media. As for the Islamic
Republic of Iran, the very identity and purpose of its leadership under the mullahs is tied to a specific Shiite fundamentalist concept of Islam and that defines
itself in opposition to "arrogance," that is, American hegemony. Moreover, the
regime commands not only the security services, military, and judiciary, but
also the powerful Iranian Revolutionary Guard Corps (IRGC) and the Basij
people's militia with branches in every Iranian city. In doing so, it exercises
authority over domestic and foreign policy, even while a young and restless
population would welcome liberalization and change. And it is presided over by

[19] This discussion summarizes the analysis by Gilbert Rozman in, "Asia for the Asians: Why
Chinese-Russian Friendship is Here to Stay," *Foreign Affairs*, October 29, 2014. Also see
Gilbert Rozman, *The Sino-Russian Challenge to the World Order: National Identities, Bilateral
Relations, and East Versus West in the 2010s*" (Washington, DC: Woodrow Wilson Center Press
with Stanford University Press, 2014).

[20] For example, John J. Mearsheimer, "Why the Ukraine Crisis Is the West's Fault: The Liberal
Delusions That Provoked Putin," *Foreign Affairs*, Vol. 93, No. 5 (September/October 2014), pp.
77–89. For a compelling rebuttal to this argument, see Stephen Sestanovich, "Could It Have
Been Otherwise?" *The American Interest*, Vol. X, No. 5 (May/June 2015), pp. 7–15.

what strategist and diplomatic historian Michael Mandelbaum has described as an "aging, provincial, autocratic, fiercely anti-Semitic, anti-Western, and anti-American Persian cleric."[21]

The Obama approach to foreign policy not only incorporates key realist assumptions, but in its misgivings about the use of American power and emphasis on the international community and international institutions also incorporates certain beliefs of liberal internationalists. Although liberals do not share the realist enthusiasm for pulling back from global engagement, their emphasis on international institutions implies reluctance to see the United States act decisively in the absence of authorization by the UN or other international bodies. For example, although liberal internationalist scholar John Ikenberry and his coauthors have argued for the United States to continue to "lean forward" in its international engagement,[22] he also has claimed to see the emergence of an international order with "constitutional characteristics" and argued that shared needs are incentivizing countries toward closer collaboration including "an open rule-based international system" and a "demand for multilateral rules and institutions."[23] A still more ambitious argument is offered by Joseph M. Colomer, who holds that "world government actually exists." In his view, global organizations, regimes and financial bodies, not only the UN, its agencies, and international courts, but also such groupings as the G-20, the EU, various regional and functional institutions, and self-appointed directorates, already are acting in that capacity.[24] → No enforcement?

Arguments such as these put excessive faith in the capacity of international institutions to act effectively on the most urgent and deadly problems and in getting the international community to respond on a timely basis. They also tend to place disproportionate emphasis on the role of emerging powers (the BRICS) as stakeholders rather than free-riders in adapting and sustaining international order. To be sure, some liberal thinkers and policymakers have favored robust intervention under the doctrine of Responsibility to Protect (R2P) in order to combat genocide, war crimes, ethnic cleansing, and crimes against humanity in circumstances where an individual state is unable or unwilling to act or is responsible for the carnage.[25] The Libya intervention of March 2011

e.g.

Not true in reality

[21] Michael Mandelbaum, "It's the Deterrence, Stupid," *The American Interest*, July 30, 2015, www.the-american-interest.com/2015/07/30/its-the-deterrence-stupid/.

[22] Stephen G. Brooks, G. John Ikenberry, and William C. Wohlforth, "Lean Forward: In Defense of American Engagement," *Foreign Affairs* (January/February 2013), pp. 130–142.

[23] John Ikenberry, "The Future of the Liberal World Order: Internationalism after America," *Foreign Affairs* (May–June 2011), pp. 56–68.

[24] Josep M. Colomer, *How Global Institutions Rule the World* (New York: Palgrave Macmillan, 2014), p. 3.

[25] That is, the Responsibility to Protect, a doctrine approved by the United Nations in UN Security Council Resolutions 1674 (2006) and 1894 (2009). This holds that the duty to prevent and halt genocide and mass atrocities lies first with the State, but the international community has a role that cannot be blocked by the invocation of sovereignty. Thus sovereignty no longer

was the most conspicuous case of this, though the subsequent chaos in Libya and the difficulty of gaining approval from the UN Security Council including Russia and China make future interventions of this kind unlikely.

RETRENCHMENT IN PRACTICE

Some observers have questioned whether an Obama Doctrine really exists at all. Obama himself has downplayed the need for an overarching foreign policy concept, and he has been quoted in describing his own approach as, "Don't do stupid [stuff]." Nonetheless there is good reason to argue that an Obama Doctrine does exist and that the hallmarks of it include the elements cited above: retrenchment and disengagement, a deep wariness about the exercise of American power, conciliatory policies toward adversaries, a distancing from traditional allies (notable too in the absence of a positive personal relationship with any of their leaders), an emphasis on the international community and multilateral organizations over autonomous American initiatives, and a focus on domestic affairs.[26] → "Obama Doctrine"

To be sure, this preference for "leading from behind"[27] did not preclude selective use of force. Despite the aversion to providing combat troops ("boots on the ground") there was a significant increase in the use of remotely piloted drone aircraft for targeted assassinations and attacks on terrorist targets. Special Forces units were also employed in operations, as in the killing of Osama bin Laden in May 2011. In addition, military advisers have operated training missions in scores of countries, and after the major inroads made by ISIS in Syria and Iraq, US military aircraft began targeted attacks in both countries. Indeed, in seeking to rebut comments that the administration was too diffident about the use of force, one senior official proclaimed privately, "We kill people all the time."[28]

In practice, as in the case of Syria, vacillation and policy reversals – including early support for moderate rebels that was never forthcoming and proclamation of a "red line" that was later abandoned after Assad used chemical weapons – fed widespread uncertainty about the Obama administration's resolve, credibility, and even competence. In the case of Ukraine, the initial Obama response signaled that the United States would do little beyond economic sanctions to counter Moscow's invasion of a European country. Moreover, even at the diplomatic level, the Obama response was often minimal. The avoidance shown by the United States in the Middle East and Europe caused regional actors to

exclusively protects States from foreign interference. See www.un.org/en/preventgenocide/adviser/responsibility.shtml.

[26] The Obama Doctrine is treated at length in Chapter 5.

[27] The widely quoted words of an Obama insider, describing policy toward the Libyan intervention in spring 2011, in Ryan Lizza, "The Consequentialist: How the Arab Spring Remade Obama's Foreign Policy," *The New Yorker*, May 2, 2011.

[28] Conversation with the author, April 30, 2015.

hedge against abandonment by Washington, thus making present or future cooperation more difficult and damaging American credibility among allies as well as adversaries.

Arguments for retrenchment and disengagement, whether from policymakers, realist thinkers or liberal internationalists tend to undervalue the wide range of options between nonintervention and war and to downplay the costs of inaction. Aversion to the use of power and a downplaying of the military component of foreign policy can undercut the effectiveness of diplomacy. Rhetoric that proclaims a stark binary choice between diplomacy and war can itself be shortsighted and unrealistic. In practice, it is often a rationale for inaction and undercuts diplomacy itself. Rather than representing polar opposites, skillful wielding together of the two is crucial. Diplomacy tends to be far more effective when backed by power and the will to use it. The combination of these tools of foreign policy strengthens the effectiveness of deterrence, reassures allies, and can lessen the need to utilize military power.

In recent years, rather than enhancing America's own security and national interests, retrenchment has coincided with heightened instability and disorder, expanding civil wars, growing territorial control by hostile actors, confrontational policies by regional powers, increased threats from terrorism, mounting refugee problems, weapons proliferation, and appalling abuses of human rights. This experience lends support to a broader argument about the importance of a more robust American role, not only to serve its own national interests, but to sustain regional and global order as well.

2

Burden sharing with Europe

Problems of capability and will

[T]he Americans hardly play a role any more [in Europe]
— Sueddeutsche Zeitung[1]

With the end of the Cold War, the liberation and democratization of Eastern Europe, and the subsequent expansion and deepening of the EU, there were widely shared expectations throughout the 1990s that a united Europe of 500 million people would soon become a truly major power in world affairs and a model for the rest of the world. That was then. With the passage of time, the spread of globalization, and the rise of China and BRICS, the relative influence of America's longtime allies, Europe and Japan, has eroded as these traditional centers of power have experienced economic and demographic stagnation. Europe today remains less than the sum of its parts, faces deep structural and political divisions, possesses rapidly declining military forces, and lacks both the capability and political will to address the most urgent and important problems of world order. At the same time, the Atlantic partnership has weakened as the United States has downplayed its European commitments and Europeans themselves have become less capable and more inclined to hedge their bets. As a consequence, the centrality of the United States in sustaining that order has increased, even as America's own engagement has lessened and its relative standing is challenged.

To understand what has happened and why, it is important to reexamine the initial post–World War II era of American leadership and European development, the widely shared post–Cold War vision for Europe's future and global order, and the impact of globalization and changing demography on Europe and Japan.

---

[1] Chief Editor, Karl Kister, quoted in John Vinocur, "Putin Begins to Crack the Atlantic Alliance," *Wall Street Journal*, February 17, 2015.

THE COLD WAR ERA AND GLOBAL ORDER

For more than half a century the advanced industrial democracies established and sustained international institutions and global order. The "trilateral" powers (North America, Western Europe, and Japan) served as the pillars of that order, which included not only the United Nations, but functional and regional organizations encompassing, *inter alia,* economics, monetary policy, trade, investment, development, health, human rights, aviation, communications, security, and international law.

In retrospect, this may seem a halcyon period, with rapid economic growth and rising living standards, expansion of shared institutions, and cooperation under American Cold War leadership. But collaboration among these powers was by no means seamless, and though it may appear otherwise, there was no shortage of disputes among them over issues large and small. From 1950 onward there were periodic but often intense disagreements over military and defense issues, trade, economic policy, the role of the dollar, energy, burden sharing, and strategies for dealing with the Soviet Union. Indeed, as early as 1965, Henry Kissinger could write a book about the tensions in US–European relations and title it, *The Troubled Partnership.*[2]

A number of these disputes seemed at the time to shake the entire relationship. In the early 1950s, proposals for creation of a European Army and German rearmament triggered angry recriminations across the Atlantic and within Europe itself. In 1956, the British–French invasion of Suez caused a temporary rupture with Washington when the Eisenhower administration condemned the operation and voted with the USSR in the UN Security Council. The American action caused deep resentment in France and Britain, as it illuminated their reduced global status and rapidly fading imperial roles.[3] During the 1960s, Soviet attainment of nuclear parity with the United States triggered anxieties about the credibility of American security guarantees.[4] In 1971, President Richard Nixon responded to rising balance of payments deficits and pressure from French President Charles de Gaulle by closing the gold window (i.e., halting the convertibility of the dollar to gold at $35 per ounce), in effect ending the relationship between currencies and the price of gold and with it the Bretton Woods system of fixed exchange rates that had been in place since 1945.

---

[2] Henry A. Kissinger, *The Troubled Partnership: A Re-Appraisal of the Atlantic Alliance* (New York: McGraw-Hill, 1965).

[3] See, for example, Herman Finer, *Dulles over Suez: The Theory and Practice of His Diplomacy* (Chicago: Quadrangle Books, 1964).

[4] For one of the earliest and arguably the most cogent analysis of the problem of extended deterrence, see Raymond Aron, *Le Grand Debat: Initiation a la strategie atomique* (Paris: Calmann-Levy, 1963), in English, *The Great Debate: Theories of Nuclear Strategy* (Garden City, New York: Anchor Books, 1965).

e.g. The October 1973 Yom Kippur War and Arab oil embargo led to strident disagreements among NATO allies. All but Portugal refused to allow refueling for American aircraft carrying desperately needed military supplies to Israel, and deep differences erupted over Middle East policy, energy, and the role of OPEC. The decade also saw disagreement about Germany's *Ostpolitik*, its policy of detente toward the Soviet Union and Eastern Europe. In the early 1980s the Euromissile dispute over the NATO basing of intermediate range nuclear missiles to counter comparable Soviet weapons in Eastern Europe triggered violent demonstrations by antiwar protestors in Western Europe, some of whose support came from covert involvement by East German and Russian security services.

Meanwhile, during the decades of the 1970s and 1980s, Japan's dynamic economy and rapid export-led growth made it an increasingly formidable economic force. Worries began to be expressed in Western capitals about Japanese competition and investments as well as about an increasingly powerful Japan potentially distancing itself from the United States. A leading Harvard specialist, Ezra Vogel, authored a widely cited book entitled, *Japan as Number One: Lessons for America*.[5] In turn influential Japanese leaders wrote about *The Japan That Can Say No: Why Japan Will Become First Among Equals*.[6] In it, Akito Morita, the former head of the Sony Corporation proclaimed, "We are going to have an entirely new configuration in the balance of power in the world." His colleague, a leading politician, Shintaro Ishihara, added, "There is no hope for the U.S."[7]

In light of more than two decades of Japanese economic stagnation that followed, anxieties about its power and its potential threat to the United States seem a curious relic. But at the time, even a prominent, sober-minded strategist such as Samuel Huntington could express deep concerns about Japan. In his words, "Japanese strategy is a strategy of economic warfare."[8]

Throughout those years, America's allies, but especially the Europeans, chafed at US leadership, complaining when it was too much – or too little. Nonetheless, postwar European order, and with it an international economic order, became consolidated and durable. At the same time, in what was still the Cold War context and its immediate aftermath, there was a sufficient sense of common purpose to prevent the differences among America, Europe, and Japan – the advanced market democracies – from getting out of hand.

↳ wanted cooperation

[5] Ezra Vogel, *Japan as Number One: Lessons for America* (Cambridge, MA: Harvard University Press, 1979).

[6] Shintaro Ishihara, *The Japan That Can Say No: Why Japan Will Become First Among Equals* (New York: Simon & Schuster, 1991).

[7] Quoted, Flora Lewis, "Foreign Affairs: Japan's Looking Glass," *New York Times*, November 8, 1989.

[8] The quote and warnings about Japan's rising influence can be found in Samuel H. Huntington, "Why International Primacy Matters," *International Security*, Vol. 17, No. 4 (Spring 1993), pp. 68–93, at pp. 75–80.

A POST–COLD WAR VISION: EUROPE AND GLOBAL ORDER

With the end of the Cold War, the momentous events of 1989–91, and the collapse of the Soviet Union, the European continent and the international system appeared to be at a profound turning point. The United States began a long, steady drawdown of its troop levels, while Europe itself was being transformed. German unification, formally concluded on October 3, 1990, was accompanied by agreement to widen, deepen, and intensify the scope of economic and political integration. The purpose of doing so was not only to advance European unity, but to permanently enmesh an expanded and newly powerful Germany in a web of shared institutions.

The Maastricht Treaty of 1992 transformed the existing twelve country European Community into the new European Union (EU). The Treaty provided for a full economic and monetary union, a common foreign policy, and a common currency – ultimately the Euro – to be shared by most member states except Britain and Denmark who had opted out. Over the next two decades, the EU expanded, adding Austria, Finland, and Sweden in 1995, then enlarging to its East and South, taking in not only former Communist countries of Eastern Europe, but also the former Soviet Baltic republics as well as others including several Balkan countries.

For many scholars, pundits, and politicians, events surrounding the end of the Cold War signaled that traditional issues of conflict and war had become outmoded and that "new issues" of international affairs and world order would take their place. Francis Fukuyama's ideas in his *End of History*, celebrating the triumph of liberal democracy and the market economy, were emblematic, and they were widely shared and even heralded, though Samuel Huntington's *Clash of Civilizations* expressed a darker, more pessimistic vision.[9]

EUROPE IN THE CHANGING *POST* POST–COLD WAR WORLD

On the threshold of the twenty-first century, the EU seemed destined to become a major actor in the international system. Though almost all of its member countries remained allied with the United States within NATO and it did not aspire to be a formidable military power on the scale of the Americans, the EU with its then fifteen member countries appeared to be emerging with an influential global role of its own. America was respected for its size, power, and dynamism, but it was also resented for the same reasons, as evident in French foreign minister Hubert Vedrine's widely quoted complaint about its "hyperpuissance" (hyperpower). Vedrine decried rising US predominance in all

---

[9] Francis Fukuyama, "The End of History," *The National Interest*, Vol. 16. (Summer 1989), pp. 3–18; and *The End of History and the Last Man* (New York: Free Press, 1992); Samuel Huntington, "The Clash of Civilizations? *Foreign Affairs*, Vol. 72 No. 3 (Summer 1993), pp. 22–49, and *The Clash of Civilizations and the Remaking of World Order* (New York: Simon & Schuster, 1996).

categories, extending beyond economics, technology, or military might to "this domination of attitudes, concepts, language and modes of life."[10] A more positive reaction came in the awed assessment of Britain's Paul Kennedy. Writing in the *Financial Times* following his visit to a US Navy aircraft carrier, the author of *The Rise and Fall of the Great Powers* exclaimed:

Nothing has ever existed like this disparity of power; nothing ... Charlemagne's empire was merely Western European in its reach. The Roman empire stretched farther afield, but there was another great empire in Persia, and a larger one in China. There is therefore no comparison.[11]

The contrasting vision for Europe at the time was one of a peaceful, prosperous, rule-based body with a powerful voice in world affairs including not only economic, monetary, trade, energy, and environmental policy, but also foreign policy, human rights, and moral leadership. The following years did see an impressive enlargement and deepening of Europe's institutions. In 2002 the Euro came into existence as an actual currency. In 2004 the EU added ten new members, mostly from Eastern Europe (Cyprus, Czech Republic, Estonia, Hungary, Latvia, Lithuania, Malta, Poland, Slovakia, and Slovenia). In 2007 Bulgaria and Romania joined, and in 2013 Croatia brought the total membership to twenty-eight countries.

The vision of a peaceful, orderly post–Cold War Europe as a model for the world had previously been shaken, though not disrupted, by conflicts in the Balkans (Bosnia 1992–5 and Kosovo 1999), but in the years after the 9/11 terrorist attacks on New York and Washington, Europe's own problems became increasingly apparent and relations with the United States became more fraught. Initially the European allies had rallied to support the United States. They invoked the mutual security provisions of the North Atlantic Treaty's Article 5 for the first time in the alliance's history and sent troops to fight alongside the Americans in Afghanistan as part of the NATO-led International Security Assistance Force (ISAF) established by the UN Security Council. Subsequently, on the eve of the Iraq War, some two-thirds of the presidents or prime ministers of the NATO and EU member countries endorsed the Bush administration's use of force. Of these, eight mainly Western European leaders signed a support letter written by British Prime Minister Tony Blair and Spanish President Aznar.[12] In addition ten heads of Eastern and Southern European countries, the Vilnius group, endorsed a similar statement.[13]

---

[10] French Foreign Minister Hubert Vedrine, quoted in "To Paris, U.S. Looks Like a 'Hyperpower'," *New York Times*, February 5, 1990.

[11] Paul Kennedy, "The Eagle Has Landed," *Financial Times* (London), February 1, 2002.

[12] The Blair and Aznar letter was signed by the leaders of the Czech Republic, Denmark, Hungary, Italy, Poland, and Portugal. It was published in *The Times* (London), under the title, "Europe and America Must Stand United," January 30, 2003. The US-led war in Iraq, known as Operation Iraqi Freedom (OIF), began on March 19, 2003.

[13] The Vilnius group included Albania, Bulgaria, Croatia, Estonia, Latvia, Lithuania, Macedonia, Romania, Slovakia, and Slovenia. Their statement appeared on February 5, 2003. See "Eastern

However, the Iraq War soon became the subject of bitter disagreement between Washington and many of its European partners. It also became a catalyst for what some observers saw as a potential global leadership role for the EU, distinct from or even balancing against the United States. The leaders of France, Germany, and Belgium became vocal opponents of the war, joining Russia in their strident criticism of the Bush administration's actions. European public opinion turned sharply against the United States and it became increasingly commonplace among pundits, policymakers, and journalists to foresee a profound rupture in the long-standing Atlantic relationship.

French President Jacques Chirac was the most outspoken among European opponents of American policy at the time, and the criticisms extended well beyond Iraq. In his words, "Any community with only one dominant power is always a dangerous one and provokes reactions. That's why I favor a multipolar world in which Europe obviously has its place."[14] He then widened the breach, adding that, "we need a means to struggle against American hegemony."[15] Chirac was by no means alone in his views; German Chancellor Gerhard Schroeder was similarly critical, and the former head of the European Commission, Italian diplomat Romano Prodi, observed that a chief goal for the EU was to create "a superpower on the European continent that stands equal to the United States."[16] In turn, some American scholars predicted the collapse of NATO. Kenneth Waltz wrote that "NATO's days are not numbered, but its years are."[17] And Charles Kupchan (who a dozen years later went on to serve as a senior director for European policy on the Obama National Security Council) wrote that "NATO, far from being in the midst of a rejuvenation, is soon to be defunct."[18]

Though the years from 2003 to 2006 were a period of turmoil in Atlantic relations, a rupture did not occur, not least because of continuing and shared interests. These included not only long-standing economic and political priorities, but also security issues and the threat of terrorism. The Europeans themselves experienced bloody attacks, notably the Madrid train bombings in March 2004 and the London bus and underground attacks of July 2005. Most

Europe: Vilnius Group Supports U.S. On Iraq," Radio Free Europe, Radio Liberty, www.rferl .org/content/article/1102148.html, accessed March 12, 2015.

[14] Chirac interview, *Time* magazine, February 24, 2003.

[15] Quoted in *The Economist*, April 24, 2003.

[16] *Ibid.*

[17] Kenneth Waltz, "The Emerging Structure of International Politics," *International Security*, Vol. 18, No. 2 (Fall 1993), pp. 75–76.

[18] Charles A. Kupchan, "The Waning Days of the Atlantic Alliance," in Bertel Heurlin and Mikkel Vedby Rasmussen, eds., *Challenges and Capabilities: NATO in the 21st Century* (Copenhagen: Danish Institute for International Studies, 2003), p. 25. Kupchan also wrote that the EU would emerge within the decade to counterbalance the United States; see Charles A. Kupchan, *The End of the American Era: U.S. Foreign Policy and the Geopolitics of the Twenty First Century* (New York: Knopf, 2002).

European governments understood the importance of retaining close working relations with the United States, and even the French continued to collaborate actively with Washington on important economic and security matters including counterterrorism. With the outbreak of the great financial crisis in 2008–9, close cooperation between Europe and the United States was essential. In addition, the end of the Bush presidency and the coming to office of the Obama administration brought a major change in European public opinion.

WHAT'S WRONG WITH EUROPE?

In the middle of the second decade of the twenty-first century, the EU and many of its member countries find themselves weakened, debellicized, in disarray internally, and facing public backlash. Instead of flourishing as once widely anticipated, Europe remains less than the sum of its parts, lacking both the capability and political will to address its own most urgent problems let alone those of world order. Despite the rhetoric that has accompanied the widening and deepening of the EU and the aspirational language of its founding documents and treaties, it remains far short of a true political union and thus without a meaningful common defense and foreign policy that such a union would enable.

NB

These weaknesses have been evident in a deepening refugee crisis, as vast numbers of desperate people have sought to cross the Mediterranean to reach Greece and Italy, or travel overland via Turkey, Greece, the Balkans, and Hungary. Many seek entry to the prosperous welfare states of Northern Europe, especially Germany and Sweden. They are among the many millions fleeing from violence and war in Syria, Iraq, Libya, Yemen, Afghanistan, and Somalia, but there are also many others from North Africa, the Sahel, Bangladesh, and Pakistan pursuing economic opportunity. Millions have taken refuge in Turkey, Jordan, and Lebanon, but many others embark on a dangerous effort to reach Europe. Recipient countries have become overwhelmed, thousands of refugees have died at sea, and others have perished while crammed into locked trucks or on the arduous overland voyage. In responding, the Europeans have found themselves in disarray, not only without an effective refugee policy, but lacking the capacity to intervene at the source – whether through diplomatic, economic, political, or military means. *→ huge problem facing EU now*

In 2015 alone, more than 1.1 million migrants entered Germany; 160,000 arrived in Sweden, and substantial numbers came to Denmark, the Netherlands, and other countries of Northern Europe. In the face of this human crisis, with EU members unable to agree upon or implement an effective common policy, individual countries began taking their own measures to restrict entry. Among these, recipient countries such as Denmark, the Netherlands, Finland, and Austria sought to become much more selective or to limit new admissions altogether, while transit countries including Slovakia, Croatia, and Hungary erected barbed wire barriers at their borders.

⤷ Tensions are high as shown by support for conservative, right-wing policies — Brexit etc.

refugee crisis

successes

Nonetheless, despite increasingly serious problems, it is important to keep in mind that Europe has been transformed in the course of the past seven decades. For three centuries, between the Peace of Westphalia in 1648, which ushered in the European nation-state system, and the end of World War II, Europe was the focal point of interstate and great power conflict and war. This culminated in the catastrophes of the twentieth century, among them World War I, Soviet Communism, Nazism, World War II, and the Holocaust. Since that time, at least in so far as the twenty-eight EU member countries of Western and Central Europe are concerned, Europe has become a security community, in which the member states no longer prepare for or even consider the possibility of war against one another.[19] Moreover, the breadth, scope, and accomplishments of the EU should not be underestimated. It has successfully created common institutions for many domestic functions of government, removed barriers to trade, investment, and – at least until the impact of the refugee crisis – the free movement of people, and played a valuable role in the transformation of Southern and Eastern European countries that were once military dictatorships or Communist tyrannies. Its strengths include not only the expanse of its membership and population of 508 million,[20] but also a $17 trillion economy almost as large as that of the United States, as well as the importance of its regulatory role, and its presence as a sometime diplomatic partner in international negotiations and institutions.

huge achievement

Recession & economy

Yet Europe suffers from deep-seated economic, social, and political problems. The causes of these are both internal and external, and they have the effect of diminishing the EU's overall strength as well as its effectiveness in sustaining world order. The first and most immediate of Europe's problems is that of economic performance. Measured in total Gross Domestic Product (GDP), the nineteen countries of the Eurozone (and Japan) have yet to regain their pre-financial crisis peak of early 2007.[21] Still worse, unemployment remains stubbornly high at more than 10.5 percent of the labor force. Youth unemployment averages 21.5 percent and in some of the most severely affected economies (Greece, Spain, and Portugal) it is far higher. These numbers also mask deep differences among member countries. Britain, Sweden, Denmark, the Netherlands, and Poland are performing relatively better than most of their EU counterparts. Germany's economy has become the largest and most successful in Europe, its unemployment rate at 6.2 percent (January 2016) is far

---

[19] The term *security community*, is that of the late political scientist. Karl W. Deutsch. See Karl W. Deutsch, Sidney A. Burrell, Robert A. Kann, and Maurice Lee Jr., *Political Community and the North Atlantic Area: International Organization in the Light of Historical Experience* (Princeton, NJ: Princeton University Press, 1957).

[20] Figure for EU population in 2015. Source, Eurostat, www.tradingeconomics.com/european-union/population.

[21] "Eurozone" includes the nineteen EU countries using the Euro currency. See *Outlook: U.S. Preeminence*, Investment Management Division, Goldman Sachs, January 2015, Exhibit 4, p. 8, www.goldmansachs.com/our-thinking/trends-in-our-business/us-preeminence.html.

below the EU's average, and its 2015 trade surplus of some $250 billion was second only to that of China.

The causes of Europe's lagging economic performance are a matter of intense debate. Some critics, especially on the political left, have blamed austerity policies put in place to cope with large domestic budget deficits resulting from the 2008–9 financial crisis and great recession. German leaders and many mainstream economists, however, focus on excessive government spending, costly social programs, and the lack of structural reform, especially in Southern Europe. They point to rigid labor markets, laws that make it hard to lay off unneeded workers, and regulatory barriers to entrepreneurship and many professional occupations.

Many European countries have also failed to put the costs of their elaborate welfare states on a sustainable long-term basis. As German Chancellor Angela Merkel is fond of remarking, Europe represents 7 percent of the world's population, 25 percent of its GDP, and 50 percent of its welfare spending. The Eurozone crisis brought these problems to a head, especially among a group of countries, Portugal, Italy, Ireland, Greece, and Spain (the "PIIGS") that came close to financial collapse. Having adopted the Euro at fixed exchange rates, and for the most part having failed to carry out structural and budgetary reforms, they lacked the policy tool of currency devaluation to which they might otherwise have resorted.

In this regard, Germany's enormous balance of trade surplus makes the plight of its weaker EU partners still more difficult. As former Federal Reserve Chairman Ben Bernanke observed, Germany in 2014 had not only the world's largest trade surplus in absolute terms, but also as a share of its GDP, at almost 7 percent. In comparison, China's surplus as a percentage of its much larger GDP was approximately 3 percent. The International Monetary Fund (IMF) calculates that due to Germany's membership in the Euro its inflation-adjusted exchange rate is effectively undervalued. This provides a cost advantage for German exports and, as Bernanke notes, "The fact that Germany is selling so much more than it is buying redirects demand from its neighbors as well as from other countries, reducing output and employment outside Germany at a time when monetary policy in many countries is reaching its limits."[22]

Germany thus has benefitted mightily from the Euro, but has been reluctant to support Euro bonds and underwrite the massive monetary commitment that might enable the worst affected countries sufficient debt relief and a way out of the crisis. The core problem here was institutional. The EU had achieved monetary union, but without a true political union that would otherwise have made costly adjustment measures politically palatable.

↳ needs to be a monetary AND political union

[22] Ben S. Bernanke, "Germany's Trade Surplus Is a Problem," *Ben Bernanke's Blog, The Brookings Institution*, Washington, DC, April 3, 2015, www.brookings.edu/blogs/ben-bernanke/posts/2015/04/03-germany-trade-surplus-problem.

Demography

Beyond the Eurozone crisis, Europeans have a more fundamental problem – demography. With aging populations, and early and often mandatory retirement requirements, European dependency ratios are worsening. These measure the relationship between the percentage of those in the active workforce versus the figure for those (children, the aged, and the disabled) who need to be supported. Moreover, European birth rates mostly languish far beneath the ratio required for avoiding population decline: a total fertility rate (TFR), the average number of children born to a woman during her lifetime, of 2.1.[23]

This decline in fertility rates has been remarkably sudden, especially for predominantly Catholic countries where the change has occurred in the course of one generation. Thus Spain's rate has fallen to 1.40 and Italy's to 1.43. Economic performance is likely to have some effect, but Germany despite its low unemployment figures has a TFR of just 1.44. Culture, social change, wider availability of birth control, and expanding opportunities for women in modern societies may also contribute to low birth rates. Based on international comparisons, most middle- or high-income countries are experiencing similar problems. The effect is especially evident in East Asia, where Japan's figure is a low 1.40 and its neighbors such as South Korea, Singapore, and Hong Kong have comparable TFRs. China's rate is 1.56, with some of that attributable to its notorious one-child policy. Socioeconomic factors do not, however, provide a complete explanation, given the differences among otherwise comparable countries. The TFR for France, in part due to its expansive neonatal, family, and child care policies, is 1.94, while the United States, with less generous social provisions, nonetheless has a TFR of 2.06.

Technological change and globalization also play a part in Europe's economic performance. The rise of Japan and the "Asian Tigers" in the 1970s and 1980s, with their export-led growth strategies, brought intense economic competition, especially in foreign markets. Although Japan's performance has lagged in recent decades, the impact of China, with its comparatively low labor costs, massive scale, and predatory investment, technology, and trade policies has been enormous, especially since its admission to the World Trade Organization in 2001. Some countries, such as Britain with its advantage in financial services, Germany in high-end manufacturing, France in nuclear power and high-speed trains, and Italy in specialized luxury products retain important areas of competitiveness, but Europe's overall problem remains that of supporting expensive welfare states and the attractive way of life they make possible.

[23] Estimated total fertility rates as of 2015: United States 2.06, France 1.94, United Kingdom 1.89, Netherlands 1.78, Sweden 1.67, Spain 1.40, Germany 1.44, Italy 1.43, Japan 1.40, and Poland 1.34. The leading revisionist powers also exhibited TFR numbers well below replacement: Iran 1.83, Russia 1.45, and China 1.56. Source: Geoba.se: Gazetteer – The World – Total Fertility Rate – Top 100+ By Country (2015), www.geoba.se/population.php?pc=w orld&page=2&type =010&st=rank&asde=&year=2015.

Throughout much of the continent, economic anxieties and the complex impact of globalization have affected domestic politics. As the EU has expanded and taken on more and more control of functions once exclusively the responsibility of member governments, popular distrust and resentment of a distant, bureaucratic, and often unresponsive EU authority in Brussels has surged. Though the directly elected European Parliament has acquired additional authority, its members do not have a close relationship to domestic constituencies. Popular frustrations and resentments are increasingly directed against the EU, whether or not it is responsible. Moreover, widening public frustration over the migrant crisis has fostered increased resentment between member countries and toward the EU itself.

As a result of these pressures, populist parties have gained increasing attention and support. The resentments they express are aimed at domestic political and cultural elites and institutions, but especially in regard to the EU, and their targets include the flood of new immigrants as well as existing ones, especially Muslims who often have not become fully assimilated in these societies and who receive welfare benefits at prevailing European levels. Under the Lisbon Treaty, which took effect in 2009, foreigners legally residing in member countries are "entitled to social security benefits and social advantages in accordance with Union law and national laws and practices."[24]

The most visible and well known of the European populist parties is France's National Front. Initially extreme right-wing in orientation, it has thrived while discarding much of its earlier more radical and anti-Semitic elements. In doing so, it has attracted disgruntled former leftists and many others with its anti-Brussels, antimodernist, anti-immigrant arguments, and in local elections it has gained more than a quarter of the popular vote. In Britain, the UK Independence Party (UKIP), once a fringe party, has gained traction with its call for Britain to quit the EU. In the 2015 parliamentary elections, UKIP received 12.6 percent of the votes, the third largest number after the Conservative and Labour Parties. That put it well ahead of the Liberal Democrats (8 percent), Scottish Nationalist Party (4.7 percent), and Greens (3.8 percent), even though – thanks to the British single member district electoral system – it won only one seat.

Even in Germany, two iconoclastic parties have gained in public support. One is the Alternative for Germany (AfD) led by a number of economists and business professionals who are critical of the EU and its effects, and which has gained seats in several of the German states and the European Parliament. The AfD's criticism of unrestricted immigration gained it growing popularity, and by early 2016, opinion polls showed it with 12.5 percent, a figure greater than that of long-established parties such as the Greens and liberal Free Democrats. Another more populist and explicitly anti-immigrant party, Patriotic Europeans Against Islamization of the West (PEGIDA), has less of a national following. However, it

---

[24] "Charter of Fundamental Rights of the European Union," *Official Journal of the European Union*, (2010C/ 83-02), March 20, 2010, p. C83/398.

attracts significant support in parts of the former East Germany and draws large crowds at anti-immigrant rallies it organizes.

Some of the other European populist parties, notably the National Front in France, Jobik in Hungary, and the neofascist Golden Dawn in Greece, in their anti-establishment, nationalist, and anti-modernist themes, express solidarity less with the Atlantic community than with Russia and its increasingly authoritarian, reactionary, and demagogic leader, Vladimir Putin. The National Front, for example, received a $10 million loan from a bank closely affiliated with the Kremlin.[25]

military

Europe's military weakness also has become increasingly apparent. In the quarter-century since the end of the Cold War, NATO countries have been asked to spend 2 percent of GDP on defense, though few of them have done so. In the aftermath of Russia's invasion of Ukraine its twenty-eight members reaffirmed that goal, but other than the United States, at 3.4 percent of GDP, only a handful of NATO members meet the 2 percent target. East European and Baltic countries that do feel most exposed to Russian power have been increasing their defense budgets. They include Estonia, Lithuania, Latvia, Poland, and Romania. The Netherlands, which saw 193 of its people killed in the July 2014 shoot down of MH17 over Ukraine, has committed to an increase, as has Norway, which has been the target of provocative intrusions in its air space by Russian combat aircraft. These countries, however, are an exception. The four largest European NATO countries barely meet or fall below the 2 percent target. Britain, which had been at 2.07 percent, spends barely 2.0 percent, even while raising its allocation to foreign aid in order to meet a target of 0.7 percent of GDP. France remains stable at 1.5 percent. Italy's defense budget is below 1.2 percent of GDP. And Germany is reducing its military spending to a record low 1.09 percent.[26] As another example of Europe's eroding capabilities, Belgium spends just 1 percent of its GDP on defense and three-fourths of its military budget is devoted to personnel costs, a statistic that has led one critic to describe the Belgian military as "an unusually well-armed pension fund."[27] For the major European counties, the data reflects a serious fall in actual capabilities. Britain, which has had a history of deploying well-trained and highly capable forces, has continued to make reductions in personnel and weapons. Though it retains four aging nuclear missile submarines with a total of fifty-eight Trident missiles and 160 deployed nuclear warheads, the

---

[25] The loan, from Russia's First Czech-Russian bank, was for 9 million euros. See "National Front's Russian Loans Cause Uproar in European Parliament," EurActiv.com, December 12, 2014, www .euractiv.com/sections/europes-east/national-fronts-russian-loans-cause-uproar-european- parliament-310599, accessed April 2, 2015.

[26] Denitsa Raynova and Ian Kearns, *The Wales Pledge Revisited: A Preliminary Analysis of 2015 Budget Decisions in NATO Member States* (London: European Leadership Network, February 2015), www.europeanleadershipnetwork.org.

[27] Quoted in Gideon Rachman, "Disarmed Europe Will Face the World Alone," *Financial Times*, February 18, 2013.

UK is cutting the size of its army over the course of a decade to a figure of only 82,000 by the year 2020 – its lowest level since the Crimean War (1853–6) – and it no longer deploys an aircraft carrier capable of launching fixed wing fighter aircraft. In reaction, the eminent scholar and expert on British politics, Anthony King, observing how successive government leaders still speak in the language of a world power, observed, "Since they cannot punch above their weight, they talk above it instead."[28]

Germany's military capabilities have become even more problematic, especially in view of its economic strength, which could support higher expenditures. In maneuvers for a joint NATO rapid reaction task force, a unit of German special forces was reported to have used black painted broomsticks in place of missing heavy machine guns for their armored vehicles. German forces also face serious deficiencies in available fighter aircraft, helicopters, and even night vision goggles.[29]

The erosion of Europe's military capabilities has been slowed, however, by growing concerns about threats from the Middle East, the ravages of ISIS inside and outside the region, and terrorist attacks elsewhere, especially the November 2015 massacre in Paris. As a result, France increased its own military deployments in the region and proclaimed its "war" against ISIS. In turn, Britain announced its support for France's action, added modest funding for additional weapons and special forces, and reestablished the 2 percent target for its defense budget. For its part, Germany too expressed its support for France, dispatching a frigate and reconnaissance planes in support of the military campaign against ISIS.

European reductions in defense spending had until recently stemmed from a greatly reduced sense of direct threat. While events in the Middle East, the rise of ISIS, Russia's aggression in Ukraine, and its muscle-flexing elsewhere have shaken that complacency, other factors are at work in constraining Europe's military. These include the aging populations, increased costs of social welfare and retirement programs, and budget deficits cited previously. For European leaders faced with such budget pressures, defense has been where the money is. Domestic politics also play a role. In parliamentary systems, many coalition governments include environmental or left-of-center parties that are less inclined to support the military. Moreover, cultural dispositions affect attitudes toward the use of force. Not only the end of the Cold War, but the memories of two world wars largely waged on their own soil leave many Europeans disinclined to use force or prepare for war. → Fundamental difference with U.S.

---

[28] Quoted in Steven Erlanger, "Britain Adjusts to a More Modest Global Role," *New York Times*, April 28, 2015, citing Anthony King's recent book, *Who Governs Britain?* (London: Pelican, 2015).

[29] As an example, only thirty-eight of eighty-nine fighter planes were mission capable. Rick Noack, "Germany's Army Is So Under-equipped That It Used Broomsticks Instead of Machine Guns," *Washington Post*, February 19, 2015.

This aversion to the use of force is evident in opinion surveys. For example, European publics in the major NATO countries blame Russia for the conflict in Ukraine, and many also see Russia as a military threat to its neighbors, yet there is wide reluctance to support one's own country using force to defend NATO allies against Russia. In response to the question, "If Russia got into a serious military conflict with one of its neighboring countries that is our NATO ally, do you think our country should or should not use military force to defend that country?" majorities of French, Italians, and Germans answered "should not." Germans were the most risk averse, with only 38 percent agreeing that their country should use force.[30] Yet even while Europeans are reluctant to meet this key Article 5 obligation of their North Atlantic Treaty membership, large majorities (68 percent vs 24 percent) continue to believe America would use force to defend a NATO ally under those circumstances.[31] As evidence both of this reluctance and of transatlantic cultural differences, when asked whether force is sometimes necessary to obtain justice, only 31 percent of Europeans agree, compared with 68 percent of Americans.[32]

Despite this widespread public aversion, many of the European countries have nonetheless committed modest forces to UN peacekeeping operations or to NATO missions in either combat or supporting roles. This suggests that European elites tend to be more cognizant of strategic imperatives than the public at large. These military commitments have played a significant political and symbolic role in providing a tangible sign of alliance burden sharing. In Afghanistan most European NATO members did initially send troops or support personnel and suffered combat deaths as part of the American-led coalition. Indeed, 5,000 European troops still remain there as members of NATO's "Resolute Support" mission to train, advise, and assist Afghan security forces and institutions. Yet despite the commitment of tens of thousands of European soldiers in the NATO-led International Security and Assistance Force (ISAF) and the deaths of more than a thousand of them during the years of its operation (2001 to 2014), the United States bore the brunt of the effort with 2356 deaths, or 68 percent of coalition (non-Afghan) fatalities.[33]

In the case of Libya, Britain and France led the March 2011 effort to secure UN Security Council approval of Resolution 1973 authorizing creation of a no-fly zone and "all necessary measures" to protect civilians. Both countries played a prominent role in the subsequent air strikes and related military

[30] European opinion data from Katie Simmons, Bruce Stokes, and Jacob Poushter, "NATO Publics Blame Russia for Ukrainian Crisis, but Reluctant to provide Military Aid," Pew Research Center, June 10, 2015, question 52, www.pewglobal.org/2015/06/10/nato-publics-blame-russia-for-ukrainian-crisis-but-reluctant-to-provide-military-aid/.

[31] Pew Survey question Q53, *ibid.*

[32] The survey covered twelve European countries and the United States. See *Transatlantic Trends: Key Findings 2013* (Washington, DC: German Marshall Fund of the United States, 2013), p. 6.

[33] Data for coalition deaths by nationality in Operation Enduring Freedom, 2001–2015, http://icasualties.org/oef/, accessed April 2, 2015.

action that ultimately brought down the Gaddafi regime. Denmark, Italy, and the Netherlands participated, as did a number of Gulf Arab states; however, less than one-third of NATO countries conducted airstrikes. Germany, with NATO Europe's largest economy and population, abstained in the UN vote and did not take part in military operations.

The Libya conflict also starkly demonstrated the limits of allied capabilities. While the United States led the initial action to disable Gaddafi's air defenses, President Obama sought to limit the American role, with command of the operation quickly handed to NATO. However, as the intervention continued, it became apparent that European forces lacked the military resources that the United States could bring to bear. The number and pace of their air operations soon fell short of what it had been a dozen years earlier in NATO's first war, the seventy-seven-day Kosovo air campaign in 1999. In Libya, the Europeans quickly exhausted their supplies of precision guided weapons, and they found it necessary to rely on the Americans for sophisticated reconnaissance, surveillance, intelligence, and command and control capabilities as well as for refueling aircraft and for resupply. In reaction, and in the midst of the still ongoing conflict, Defense Secretary Robert Gates delivered a stinging rebuke to a NATO gathering in Brussels. As he put it, "The mightiest military alliance in history is only 11 weeks into an operation against a poorly armed regime in a sparsely populated country – yet many allies are beginning to run short of munitions, requiring the U.S., once more, to make up the difference."[34]

Elsewhere, especially in Africa, French troops have played critical combat roles, as in Mali in 2013 against al-Qaeda-linked militias. And in the fight against ISIS in Iraq and Syria, France sent its aircraft carrier, the *Charles de Gaulle*, to the Persian Gulf, from which its fighter planes conducted combat missions. Belgium, Britain, Denmark, and the Netherlands also have undertaken airstrikes against ISIS in Iraq, though these taken together represented only one-fourth of anti-ISIS air attacks. Germany has trained Kurdish *Peshmerga* fighters and has provided weapons training to the Iraqi military. And Albania, Britain, the Czech Republic, Estonia, France, Hungary, Italy, Portugal, and Spain either provided military aid or committed troops for training purposes.[35]

COMPARISONS AND CONTRASTS WITH JAPAN

In comparison with Europe, the situation of Japan as a major market economy, liberal democracy, and ally of the United States, displays some of the same

---

[34] Secretary of Defense Robert M. Gates, "The Security and Defense Agenda (Future of NATO)," speech delivered in Brussels, Belgium, June 10, 2011, www.defense.gov/speeches/speech .aspx?speechid=1581.

[35] Derek Chollet and Steven Keil, "France's Flagship Carrier Takes the Fight to ISIS," March 13, 2015, www.realclearworld.com/articles/2015/03/13/frances_flagship_carrier_takes_the_fight_ to_isis_111038.html.

problems and dilemmas, but by no means all of them. Once seen as *the* rising economic power of the 1980s and early 1990s, Japan experienced two decades of economic stagnation. It also suffers from problematic demography with a low birth rate and an aging and declining population. Moreover, unlike Germany, it has been unable to put to rest the deep regional memories of World War II and of Imperial Japan's actions and atrocities during that time. As a result, countries that should be close regional allies, especially South Korea, have a distant and brittle relationship with Tokyo. Notably the Koreans, Taiwanese, and others have been taken aback by occasional but ill-timed visits by a number of Japanese political officials to Tokyo's Yasukuni shrine that commemorates Japan's war dead, but that also houses the ashes of major war criminals. They also view Japan's apology as insufficient in its responsibility for the "comfort women" and wartime sexual slavery.

Japan has been bound by a postwar constitution that limits its military role. However, unlike much of post–Cold War Europe, Japan's leaders, and to an increasing extent much of its public, perceive a significant security threat, in this case from China. A rising China has moved to assert greater power along its periphery and over the waters of the East and South China Seas, including areas claimed by its neighbors and even within their maritime economic zones under the Law of the Sea Treaty. As a result, Japanese opinion has become more nationalistic. Its government under Prime Minister Shinzo Abe has gained parliamentary approval to ease the constitutional limitations on Japan's military. Thus for the first time since the end of World War II, Japan has the ability to use its military in overseas conflicts. More importantly, the changes enable it to achieve closer defense cooperation with the United States, with which it has a long-standing mutual security treaty and under whose nuclear umbrella it shelters.

EUROPEAN DILEMMAS: THE CASE OF GERMANY

The situation of Germany, the most populous and economically powerful of the European countries, is central to any understanding of Europe's dilemmas and limits. With the end of the Cold War, and firmly embedded in NATO and the EU, a unified Germany found itself, for the first time in its modern history, entirely surrounded by friendly countries. Its size and strength might have enabled it to be the driving force in a newly vigorous, prosperous, and empowered Europe, but its own limitations and the shortcomings of the EU proved constraining.

One set of limitations concerned Germany's historical responsibilities for two world wars and the Holocaust. The crimes of Hitler's Third Reich not only caused utter catastrophe for its neighbors, but for Germans themselves it caused an indelible lesson that Nazism and radical nationalism had brought them vast loss of life, the destruction of their cities, mass rape by the invading Red Army, ten million of their countrymen made homeless as refugees, and profound moral opprobrium. These memories not only left Germany's neighbors wary of its power, but also acted as a powerful inhibition on Germans themselves, who became deeply opposed to war and the use of force under almost any circumstances. Characteristically, in a 2013 Transatlantic Trends Poll, only 27 percent of Germans agreed that force is sometimes necessary to secure justice.[36] This aversion to the use of force plays a part in modern Germany's habit of quietly paying large ransoms to free its citizens kidnapped by al-Qaeda affiliates, a policy also followed by many of its European neighbors, despite the fact that this practice provides a lucrative source of funding for terrorist groups as well as encouraging further hostage taking.[37]

For the postwar generation of Germans, reconciliation with West European neighbors and the United States was indispensable in the country's recovery. As a result, NATO, European economic and institutional integration, and the embrace of international order and the rule of law became central to its identity as the Federal Republic of Germany. Simultaneously, Germany (though not its truncated Communist East) accepted an historical obligation for the safety and survival of Israel.

Seven decades after the end of World War II, and with the wartime generation having passed from the scene, Germany remains subject to competing pulls of historical memory, geography, economics, and politics. In very broad terms, its choices include, first, Atlantic partnership and a close relationship with the United States. A second alternative is built on Western and Central Europe through the EU. In different versions, this European emphasis can accompany Atlantic partnership or, for some, imply a much more distinctly separate and independent Europe. Thirdly, there are choices that extend well beyond Europe or the Atlantic, and that look toward Germany's East, especially Russia and beyond, or even to a major global role through international institutions.

In creating partnership with America, the 1948–9 Berlin airlift became a crucial catalyst. It was not that the United States was at all unknown; indeed German immigrants arrived in America in massive numbers during the nineteenth and early twentieth centuries and remain the largest single nationality by origin among Americans today. But in the aftermath of World War II and the four-power allied occupation of Germany, the United States played a special role. Together with the British, the US air force not only overcame the Soviet blockade of West Berlin, but its role helped to sway public opinion favorably

---

[36] *Transatlantic Trends: Key Findings 2013.* (Washington, DC: German Marshall Fund of the United States, 2013), p. 6.

[37] "Germany Pays Millions to an al-Qaeda Affiliate for Hostages," *The American Interest*, October 17, 2014, www.the-american-interest.com/2014/10/17/germany-pays-millions-to-an-al-qaeda-affiliate-for-hostages/; *Deutsche Welle*, "Ransom Reportedly Paid to al Qaeda-linked Group for German Hostages in Philippines," www.dw.de/ransom-reportedly-paid-to-al-qaeda-linked-group-for-german-hostages-in-philippines/a-18001549, accessed April 1, 2015; and Rukmini Callimachi, "Paying Ransoms, Europe Bankrolls Qaeda Terror," *New York Times*, July 29, 2014, accessed April 1, 2015.

toward the West. In the ensuing postwar decades and as long as Germany remained divided between East and West, the Federal Republic remained closely aligned with America. Extensive public diplomacy programs fostered a wealth of educational and cultural exchanges. German teachers and students flocked to the United States, and for an entire generation of rising German leaders, their first exposure to America often came via such programs. Meanwhile, NATO troops garrisoned Germany on the front lines of the Cold War.

With the end of the Cold War, reunification, the restoration of full German sovereignty over Berlin, and the gradual passing away of the postwar generations, the intimacy of the German–US connection began to fade. Though there had been no shortage of disagreements in prior years, for example over detente with Russia, burden sharing, Euromissile deployment, and trade policy, the security imperative had prevented such differences from threatening the overall relationship. And whereas the United States once had 325,000 military personnel in Europe, many facing Soviet Warsaw Pact forces across West Germany's borders, a steady drawdown has greatly reduced the number of troops and bases. More than a quarter-century after unification, and with Germans perceiving a much reduced need for American support, disagreements about issues large and small have taken on greater significance.

The 2003 Iraq War proved especially divisive, with Germans insisting that the use of force was illegal without formal UN sanction. German public opinion about the United States, which had persistently been quite favorable, turned sharply negative and was further worsened by controversial reports concerning the US treatment of prisoners at Abu Ghraib in Iraq and Guantanamo Bay, Cuba. In turn, during the 2011 Libya crisis, the United States and leading European allies saw Germany's abstention on the UN Security Council vote authorizing the use of force as an abdication of Berlin's responsibilities. In 2013–14, Edward Snowden's dramatic revelations about secret National Security Agency (NSA) monitoring of phone and email communications, and subsequently stories about the tapping of Chancellor Angela Merkel's cell phone further damaged the relationship.

Trade, social, and cultural problems also arose. Negotiations to create the Transatlantic Trade and Investment Partnership (TTIP) have proved difficult, with many German Greens and others intensely focusing on the alleged dangers of "chlorhunchen," American chlorinated chickens, which are sanitized by the spraying of a liquid solution to prevent the spread of salmonella during processing. Others, citing the "precautionary principle" remain vehemently opposed to the introduction of GMO food products, despite the absence of scientific evidence that these cause harm to humans.

Exchange programs have also withered, as has the teaching of German language in American schools and colleges. The Clinton administration's decision in 1999 to abolish the United States Information Agency (USIA) and to fold its functions into the State Department negatively impacted the priority, funding, and operation of cultural diplomacy as a whole, and under the successive Bush and Obama presidencies, those functions remained scattered and often without effective organizational leadership. American libraries and cultural centers, which had once been vibrant facilities, hosting cultural programming and providing a window on the United States for generations of young Germans also suffered, not least because security fears after 9/11 made it more difficult to gain easy access to embassies and centers.

The United States has, in addition, served as the perennial target of peace groups, the Greens, and of far left groups and remnants of the East German communist party gathered together in the Left Party (Die Linke). America was also anathema to smaller rightist groups and neo-Nazis. Mainstream German political parties, the center-right Christian Democrats (CDU), moderate-left Social Democrats (SPD), and liberal/centrist Free Democrats (FDP) had been generally favorable toward the United States and the western values it embodied. Yet even among those Germans with a longer view and a more nuanced sense of history, favorable attitudes have eroded, not only in response to the passage of time and Germany's changing circumstances, but also due to their sense that the German model of the social market economy is preferable to that of the United States. Together with the impact of such issues as Iraq, Guantanamo, spying, and disillusion with the presidency of Barack Obama, this sense of disillusion is captured in the words of German essayist and screenwriter, Peter Schneider, "You have created a model of a savior, and now we find by looking at you that you are not perfect at all – much less you are actually corrupt, you are terrible businessmen, you have no ideals anymore."[38]

Remarkably, and despite the wide array of factors impinging upon the German–American relationship, it still retains majority support. A poll conducted by the Bertelsmann Foundation in cooperation with the Pew Research Center found 62 percent of Germans still consider the United States to be a "reliable ally" – a response more favorable than toward Britain.[39]

For Germans, European identity exists as a strong pole of attraction, either in collaboration with America or increasingly in a more distant and separate status. The heavy burden of Germany's identity can be submerged within a European context. Indeed, only in the last decade or so have young Germans felt truly comfortable with explicit expressions of German identity such as flag display and national anthem. Its 2014 victory in the soccer World Cup provided such an opportunity for Germans to express their pride unselfconsciously.

Postwar reconciliation with France had been fundamental from 1950 onward. German leaders collaborated intimately with France in the planning and creation of the European Coal and Steel Community, Common Market, European Community, European Union, and adoption of the Euro. Prior to

↳ unlike WWl & WWll

---

[38] Quoted in George Packer's profile of Angela Merkel, "The Quiet German," *New Yorker*, December 1, 2014.

[39] Cited in "Waiting for Schindler's List," *The Economist*, June 6, 2015. The survey was conducted in late February 2015.

the massive expansion of EU membership to its current twenty-eight countries, France and Germany together were the driving force behind European unity. In recent years, however, partnership with France has proved more and more inadequate. Though France – unlike Germany – possesses nuclear weapons and a seat as one of the five permanent members of the UN Security Council, in a greatly enlarged Europe it no longer possesses comparable status and resources alongside a unified and more powerful Germany. For Germans, however, this new power position has been a mixed blessing. On economic, political, and security issues, German leaders remain wary of finding themselves too far out in front of their own population and of their EU partners.

The Eurozone crisis exemplifies this concern. Chancellor Merkel was the central figure in repeated crisis negotiations, especially with trouble-plagued Greece, but on behalf of Germany she was reluctant to bear a disproportionate share of the burden in bailing out countries in trouble. This German reluctance was not only due to insisting upon structural reforms, budget balancing, and austerity, which had worked for Germany itself, but to the limits of the EU itself. While creation of the Euro enabled Germany to benefit from enormous comparative advantages within the Eurozone, the terms of the Euro's creation locked others into a rigid currency regime without the option of currency devaluation, which made it harder for them to adapt. At the same time, the absence of political union meant that Germany had no constitutional obligation to pay for the problems of others. Within Germany, public opinion was reluctant to incur massive costs in coping with the crisis, and the rise both of populist parties and wider skepticism about the EU added a further constraint on policymakers.

 Main issue of EU today

On political and security matters too, the EU's institutional weaknesses were also apparent. In reaction to Russia's actions against Crimea and invasion of Ukraine, Germany gradually stiffened its criticism and with some difficulty managed to lead Europe in adopting economic sanctions against the Putin regime. The EU also made a large financial commitment to Ukraine, contingent on Kiev implementing long overdue economic and anticorruption reforms. But unanimity among the leaders of the twenty-eight countries proved difficult, with Hungary, Greece, and Cyprus less willing to confront Moscow. In contrast, the Baltic countries and Poland, perceiving themselves as likely targets of Moscow, pressed for stronger measures. Again, in the absence of political union, Europe's common foreign and security policy (CFSP) remained more aspirational than real. This limitation weighed against the ability or willingness to provide significant defensive weapons to the Ukraine government. Economic and trade sanctions did provide leverage against Russia, but without a European army to buttress security and deterrence, Europe's effectiveness and that of Chancellor Merkel in negotiations with Putin, lacked the impact that their size, population, and economic weight might otherwise have dictated.

Some of the German reluctance to confront Russia more directly over Ukraine stemmed from yet another broad option for Germany, that of an

Eastern-oriented or more global role rather than a more strictly European or Atlantic partnership. During the nineteenth century, a potent German romanticism had flourished tapping into a deep nationalist, anti-liberal, anti-modern and anti-Semitic current of thought. The late historian George Mosse captured this in his writing about Germany and its intellectual history, and these ideas still had resonance in the early twentieth century.[40] A widely cited example can be found in the work of the celebrated author Thomas Mann, who in 1918 penned a widely read essay which argued that Germany actually stood apart from the sterile cosmopolitanism of liberal Western Europe and that its spirit and meaning actually placed it between the West and the more tradition-bound East, as in the case of Russia. Some ideas about a mythic German past took the form of virulent notions of racial purity and invocations about blood and soil and found their way into the miasma of Nazi ideology.

In postwar Germany, such notions faded, but the temptations of a separate path in reaching understandings with Russia still lingered. There were material underpinnings too: Germany's heavy dependence on Russia for oil and natural gas and the temptations of lucrative trade and investment projects, with or without the EU and regardless of sanctions. An earlier case in point was the surprise move of former Chancellor Gerhard Schroeder on leaving office in December 2005. He resigned his seat in the Bundestag and became board chairman of a Russian–German gas pipeline company, a project he had promoted while in office and a position that seemed to reflect his close relationship with Putin and the Russian government.[41]

In the case of Ukraine, given the importance of Russia as an export market and major investments there, German firms were at first reluctant to support Western sanctions aimed at Moscow. Nonetheless, the collapse of oil prices, the fall of the Russia ruble, and an increasingly inhospitable business, legal, and regulatory climate there ultimately caused wide cutbacks in new projects and investments. For example, automobile companies reduced production and closed some of their Russian assembly plants. In addition, the huge BASF company, the world's largest chemical manufacturer, canceled a major deal with Gazprom and instead decided to increase investment in the United States to take advantage of competitive labor costs and low-priced natural gas supplies.

Characteristically, German public opinion was cautious about a prominent role for Germany in sanctioning Russia, despite compelling evidence from the conflict in Ukraine. However, the July 2014 shoot down of Malaysian Airlines Flight 17 by a Russian-made missile fired from territory the Russian-backed rebels controlled had an electrifying effect within Germany. The large number of European, especially Dutch, victims resonated in a way that thousands of Ukrainian deaths had not. As a result, Chancellor Merkel was able to lead

[40] See, for example, George L. Mosse, *The Crisis of German Ideology: Intellectual Origins of the Third Reich* (London: Weidenfeld & Nicholson, 1966).
[41] "Schroeder Accepts Russian Pipeline Job," *Washington Post*, December 10, 2005.

Europe in tightening economic and energy sanctions and to do so with some three-quarters of the public supporting the measures.

As tensions with Russia increased, a group of sixty prominent German authors, public intellectuals, and businessmen published a cautionary letter in a leading German newspaper, *Die Zeit*. In their December 2014 statement, entitled, "Another War in Europe? Not in Our Name," they blamed NATO, the United States, and the West for making Russia feel threatened. They invoked the specter of a dangerous escalation of conflict, minimized the importance of Ukraine and Crimea, and urged deferring to Russia's quest for restoring its historic sphere of interest.[42] In response, a prestigious group of foreign and security policy experts published a compelling rebuttal, "Détente without Illusions."[43] They wrote, instead, that there was just one aggressor, Russia, and one victim, Ukraine. They condemned Russia's violations of the UN Charter, the Helsinki accords of 1975, and the Budapest Memorandum. Moreover, they argued that counter to the assertions of Moscow's defenders, there was no threat to Russia, and that such claims ignored NATO defense budget cuts, the cancelation of plans for antimissile installations in Poland and the Czech Republic, and the withdrawal of US troops from Europe.

Beyond the idea of an emphasis on Russia and the East as an alternative to the Atlantic or European alignments lay the concept of an ambitious global role. In its most ambitious form, it looked back to the bygone days of Germany as a rising world power in 1871, 1914, and 1939. It also drew upon the formidable performance of the German economy, the fourth largest in the world after those of the United States, China, and Japan. Yet the global option remained out of reach. With an aging population of just 81 million people, Germany lacked the underlying basis for such a role. Despite participation in at least seventeen international peacekeeping and humanitarian missions, an alternative concept based on international institutions and the UN would founder on the weakness and limits of those bodies, as well as on Germany's lack of permanent membership on the UN Security Council. More importantly, the German population has shown no appetite for a more ambitious world role, and the reductions in Germany's defense budget to barely more than 1 percent of GDP are consistent with popular sentiment.

Ironically, a major world role for Germany as the leader of a relatively advanced and prosperous EU and its half-billion people might have been an alternative, but it is precluded both by the fundamental institutional weaknesses and lack of political union within the EU, as well as by the reticence of

---

[42] "Wieder Krieg in Europa? Nicht in unserem Namen!" by Roman Herzog, Antje Vollmer, Wim Wenders, Gerhard Schröder, *et al.*, *Zeit Online*, December 5, 2014, www.zeit.de/politik/2014-12/aufruf-russland-dialog, accessed April 1, 2015. Also see Hans Kundani, "Leaving the West Behind: Germany Looks East," *Foreign Affairs*, January–February 2015, pp. 108–116.

[43] Reinhard Wolf and Gunther Hellman, "Détente without Illusions," English translation available at www.aicgs.org/issue/detente-without-illusions/, accessed April 1, 2015.

Germans themselves and a deep-seated aversion to the employment of military force. Germany thus remains wedded to its European vocation and by necessity to a continuing though troubled relationship with the United States. Its leaders thus stress Germany's "close partnership with France within a united Europe and a strong transatlantic alliance in terms of both security and economic cooperation" as "cornerstones" of its foreign policy.[44] Yet Germany's emphasis on diplomacy is undercut by the absence of power upon which effective diplomacy ultimately depends. The Atlantic connection also remains important for the United States, but Germany's constraints as well as Europe's own deficiencies limit the extent to which it, and thus Europe, can significantly contribute to sustaining the institutions of world order.

EUROPE AND A RELUCTANT USA

For half a century after World War II, America served as Europe's "pacifier."[45] Thanks to Washington's dominant role in those years, the creation of NATO in 1949, the presence of US forces, and the Cold War nuclear umbrella, the Europeans no longer needed to worry about each other. Not only was their long-standing security dilemma solved by the presence of the superpower hegemon, but the United States also provided the massive Marshall Plan aid and underwrote the political stability that galvanized Europe's economic recovery and encouraged the development of European economic and institutional integration. → U.S. was hugely NB to making EU today

Seventy years later, much of this is ancient history, mostly remembered in commemorative rituals. Over a period of time, those Europeans who were attentive to the American role and who valued a continuing partnership increasingly expressed anxieties about successive presidents who seemed to lack the experience and background of the founding postwar generation.[46] The anxieties were mostly premature. Though Presidents Carter, Reagan, Clinton, and George W. Bush came from southern or western states, their administrations generally maintained continuity in America's European policies, even after the end of the Cold War. In practice, this meant close working relationships with European leaders, and continuing assumptions about cooperating with them on a wide range of economic, political, and security issues.

Ironically, the arrival of the Obama administration brought the kind of change that had so often been expected or feared in Europe. It was ironic in

---

[44] Foreign Minister Frank Walter Steinmeier, "The DNA of German Foreign Policy," *Project Syndicate,*" February 25, 2015, www.project-syndicate.org/commentary/german-foreign-policy-european-union-by-frank-walter-steinmeier-2015-02, accessed April 1, 2015.

[45] The term originates with Josef Joffe, "Europe's American Pacifier," *Foreign Policy,* Spring 1984, pp. 64–82.

[46] Dean Acheson, one of the seminal figures in post–World War II foreign policy as a high State Department official and then Secretary of State under President Harry S. Truman, entitled his memoir, *Present at the Creation: My Years in the State Department* (New York: Norton, 1969).

the sense that Barack Obama had been lionized there during the 2008 election year as a welcome alternative to George W. Bush. As a candidate he drew massive crowds on a visit to Berlin, and public opinion polls then and in the first year of his presidency gave him rock-star levels of popularity. The evidence was not only in favorable rankings of 80 percent or more throughout most of the continent. Barely three weeks after Obama entered the White House, the Nobel Committee awarded him its Peace Prize.

In ways big and small, the Obama administration signaled that Europe would no longer be a priority. The president and his senior foreign policy officials prioritized reaching out to adversaries and sought new relations with Russia, Iran, Syria, China, and others. Obama's June 2009 speech in Cairo emphasized a new beginning with Muslims and offered an extended apologia for generations of Western policy and attitudes. Elsewhere, the "pivot to Asia," announced in October 2011 as a "rebalancing" of US policy, made explicit the change in regional focus. And at a personal level, the president failed to establish rapport with any European leader of the kind that Ronald Reagan had maintained with Margaret Thatcher or that Bill Clinton and George W. Bush enjoyed with Tony Blair. The lone exception among NATO countries was – for a time – Prime Minister Erdogan of Turkey. This personal pattern of coolness was remarked upon by European presidents and prime ministers. Illustratively, a biography of German Chancellor Angela Merkel's recounts her asking the then French President Nicolas Sarkozy, and former British Prime Minister Gordon Brown if they too found Obama "peculiar, distant and short on warmth."[47]

This de-emphasis of European allies was evident not just in rhetoric but in policy. Thus as an early gesture in his "reset" of relations with Moscow, President Obama dropped plans for antimissile installations that were to be located in Poland and the Czech Republic. The leaders of both countries had previously incurred domestic political costs in agreeing to these programs, but the cancelation was made without seriously consulting them.

Then there was the case of Syria where, on August 21, 2013, President Assad used poison gas against his own people. In response, on August 31, Obama denounced "the worst chemical attack of the 21st century" and stated, "I have decided that the United States should take military action against Syrian regime targets."[48] In his announcement Obama had stated that he would ask Congress for authorization to use force, but on September 10, he dropped the request altogether after Russia proposed an agreement for Syria to give up its chemical weapons. Meanwhile, British Prime Minister David Cameron, had agreed to

---

[47] Conversation reported in Stefan Kornelius, *Angela Merkel: The Authorized Biography* (London: Alma Books, 2013), quoted in John Vinocur, "An Evolving Merkel Doctrine," *New York Times*, June 27, 2013.

[48] Statement by the President on Syria, Office of the Press Secretary, The White House, August 31, 2013, www.whitehouse.gov/the-press-office/2013/08/31/statement-president-syria.

cooperate in the military action, despite the lack of broad support from a public wary of casualties after Afghanistan and Iraq, but after losing a vote on the issue in the House of Commons he abandoned the commitment.

A subsequent crisis in early 2014 impacted Europe much more directly. Obama's tepid response to Russian President Putin's depredations in Crimea and Ukraine, the first time since the end of World War II that European borders had been altered by military force, was viewed with concern by European leaders. Though the American president criticized Moscow, his administration was slow to offer tangible support to Ukraine. Obama's exhortation "to mobilize the international community to put pressure on Russia" and his description of Putin's actions as "19th century behavior in the 21st century" were widely seen as empty words.[49]

In an early episode, when the embattled government in Kiev desperately sought defensive weapons including body armor, night vision goggles, and antitank weapons, the United States instead provided 300,000 military rations known as meals-ready-to-eat (MREs). Though the United States did join the EU in imposing economic sanctions on Putin and key Russian leaders and businesses, Obama took a back seat in sensitive negotiations involving Russia and Ukraine. In contrast to the case of Bosnia in 1995, when the United States led a contact group with the leaders of Britain, France, Germany, and Russia, it was German Chancellor Merkel together with French President Hollande – and without either Obama or David Cameron – who met with Putin in Minsk to negotiate terms of a cease-fire. → is it just EU now capable of doing this

Another less remarked upon, but fundamentally important element of the Ukraine crisis was the unwillingness or inability of the United States, Britain, and Russia to honor their obligations under the Budapest memorandum of December 1994. In that document, Ukraine had relinquished its nuclear arsenal, became a signatory to the Nuclear Nonproliferation Treaty (NPT), and received solemn guarantees of its territorial integrity and security. France and China signed similar, though somewhat less specific documents, thus committing all five of the UN Security Council permanent members to the agreement. Nonetheless, when put to the test by Putin's aggression and clear violation of Ukrainian sovereignty and territorial integrity, these powers failed to act. Though the United States and the United Kingdom declared Russia's action a breach of its obligations under the Budapest Memorandum, they remained reluctant even to offer weapons or training to Ukraine and their words had little effect.

This case highlights a much broader reality about international order. Solemn international guarantees by themselves are not self-enforcing. What seemed firm, authoritative assurances in 1994 proved empty in 2014–15 when not backed by American power and a unified coherent Europe.

---

[49] Quoted in Ross Douthat, "Our Thoroughly Modern Enemies," *New York Times*, August 24, 2014.

The American de-emphasis of Europe, sometimes subtle, but increasingly evident, has had other effects on the continent. At one level, it has occasioned scathing comments and offhand remarks by European officials. For example, in February 2015, Polish Foreign Minister Radek Sikorski angrily described his country's ties with Washington as "worthless."[50] It was a remarkable statement of disillusionment, given the historic affinity of Poland for the United States. Similarly, the influential editor of one of Germany's most important newspapers, the *Sueddeutsche Zeitung*, wrote that "[T]he Americans hardly play a role any more [in Europe]."   → U.S. putting an end to free riding

At another level, America's reticence has increased the propensity for the Europeans to hedge in their commitments and strategies. A major case in point is the breaking of ranks by European countries in disregarding Obama administration pleas in order to join the Chinese-sponsored Asian Infrastructure Investment Bank (AIIB). American concerns included labor, environmental, and anticorruption standards, as well as maintaining clean government safeguards required by the World Bank, Asian Development Bank, and IMF for countries receiving development loans. Moreover, the AIIB is a direct competitor to existing institutions established under American leadership as an outgrowth of the Bretton Woods conference in 1944. From China's perspective, the failure of Congress to ratify IMF reforms that would provide Beijing with a voting weight closer to its actual share in the world economy provided an impetus. The IMF countries had reached an agreement in 2010 that provided for China's voting percentage to rise from 3.8 percent to 6 percent (as contrasted with 16.5 percent for the United States), but Congress subsequently failed to pass legislation to implement the reform. Regardless of the motivation however, China's establishment of the AIIB is part of a strategy to create new international institutions enhancing its own influence.

More than two dozen Asian countries agreed to become founding members of the AIIB, and from March 2015 onward they were joined by most European countries, led by Britain and then swiftly followed by France, Germany, Italy, Switzerland, Turkey, and others. Additional members included not only Russia, but also India and America's Asian allies such as South Korea, and Australia. By the time of the Bank's formal opening in May 2015, it had gathered fifty-seven "founding" members. Notably, Japan was the lone major ally who chose to stand by the United States and forego AIIB membership. Prime Minister Shinto Abe emphasized Japan's strategic reasoning. In his words, "The United States now knows that Japan is trustworthy."[51] Unlike most of post–Cold War Europe, Japan does perceive a major security threat, in this case from China, sufficient to keep it solidly aligned with Washington.

[50] Quoted in Kori Schake, "How to Lose Friends and Allies," *Foreign Policy*, June 30, 2014, http://foreignpolicy.com/2014/06/30/how-to-lose-friends-and-alienate-allies/.

[51] Quoted in Martin Fackler, "Japan, Sticking with U.S., Says It Won't Join China-Led Bank," *New York Times*, March 31, 2015.

The actual operation and importance of the AIIB has yet to be seen. China agreed to provide $30 billion of the Bank's initial capital of $100 billion, with Asian and European members together contributing most of the remainder.[52] Though the capital remains less than that of the long-established Japanese-led Asian Development Bank, the AIIB's creation, together with the fact that leading US allies joined despite Washington's objections, was widely viewed as an embarrassment to the Obama administration and a significant indication of declining US influence with its European and Asian partners.[53]

European countries also are devoting a greater priority to their own national economic, trade, and investment interests. In dealing with Russia, for example, British officials were mindful not to jeopardize massive Russian financial investments in London, just as German business leaders were keen to protect their export markets. France, for its part, belatedly and with great reluctance finally canceled a deal to sell two powerful combat warships to the Russian navy, but only after having long insisted on the sanctity of contracts.[54]

The implication of these events is sobering. The rules, norms, institutions, and international laws that are so widely embraced as an alternative to the old geopolitics and the great conflicts of the twentieth century are not an effective substitute for national power and resolve. These require active American participation and European engagement and burden sharing. But in circumstances where the United States has downplayed its European engagements and Europeans themselves have become less capable and more inclined to hedge their bets, the future of the Atlantic partnership and of long-established international institutions and regimes is far from assured.

CAN THE PARTNERSHIP RECOVER?

If Europe and Japan have become less firm pillars of international order than they seemed a generation ago, it nonetheless remains worth asking under what conditions they, together with the United States, might instead regain much of the relative strength and influence they once possessed. There is an imperfect analogy here with discussions of American decline. Periodically, from the 1930s to the present, there have been portentous forecasts that the power and vitality of the United States were fading and that its decline in relative and even absolute terms was at hand. Assessments such as these were common during

---

[52] Mark Magnier, "China Holds Effective Control in New Bank," *Wall Street Journal*, June 8, 2015.

[53] See, for example, Andrew Higgins and David Sanger, "3 European Powers Say They Will Join China-Led Bank," *New York Times*, March 18, 2015; and "China's New Development Bank Bodes Poorly for the U.S.," *Washington Post*, March 22, 2015.

[54] French insistence on the sanctity of signed contracts was not without historical contradiction. In 1967, President Charles de Gaulle dramatically reversed French policy toward Israel and in the period before the Six Day War, his government refused to deliver fifty warplanes for which the Israelis had already paid in full.

the Great Depression, but disappeared after America entered World War II and then emerged as an unprecedented superpower. In less dramatic ways, however, predictions of decline have become cyclical, recurring in times of economic or political trouble, and then receding with recovery. The list includes, for example, reactions to the Russian launch of Sputnik in 1957, the oil shock of 1973–4, withdrawal from Vietnam in 1975, the Iranian Revolution in 1979 with US diplomats held hostage for 444 days, the Soviet Union's supposed advantage in the "correlation of forces" at the beginning of the 1980s, the predicted role of Japan as Number One later in the same decade, the financial crisis and great recession of 2008–10, and the contemporary challenge of a rising China. In each case, the United States has proved far more resilient than assumed during periods of domestic or international trouble.

In the case of Europe, what might serve to rejuvenate it and enable it to be a more capable partner? First, albeit unlikely, would be the possibility of a strong, sustained economic recovery. Despite economic, political, and demographic problems, Europe and Japan could yet achieve key structural reforms. Or they might benefit from innovative adaptations to technological change that could help to trigger renewed economic growth. Meanwhile, their foreign competitors, especially China and BRICS, could become mired in the middle income trap and see their own economic growth stagnate while the Europeans and Japanese benefit from advantages in education, their sociopolitical modernity, well-established constitutional and legal systems, and the adaptability that stable democracies can sometimes achieve.

Among the Europeans, a relaunching of regional and political integration, especially in the face of increasing adversity, is imaginable. There is precedent in that European unity has previously undergone cycles of stagnation and crisis followed by renewal and advancement. As a hint of such a possibility, European Commission President Jean-Claude Junker has proposed the creation of a European Army to show the Russians "that we are serious about defending European values."[55] This is not the first time such a concept has been offered, and less ambitious forms of military integration have taken place. For example, the Benelux countries have a common navy, the Dutch have merged their airmobile brigade into the German army's rapid reaction division, and there is a single operational command for the air transport aviation of the Benelux countries, France, Germany, and Spain.[56] Nonetheless, the obstacles to a meaningful European Army remain daunting. The British have long been opposed, other large states are divided about the idea, and its achievement would require a still highly unlikely breakthrough to a more deeply integrated European political union with characteristics of a true federal state.

[55] Duncan Robinson and James Shotter, "Jean-Claude Juncker Calls for Creation of EU Army," *Financial Times*, March 8, 2015.
[56] Jackson Janes, "A European Army: Who Speaks for Europe?" American Institute for Contemporary German Studies, www.aicgs.org, March 18, 2015.

As another possibility, the strength and economic vitality of the European–American and United States–Japan relationships could be reinvig-⑤ orated if complex trade agreements can be implemented. This would require that the Transatlantic Trade and Investment Partnership (TTIP) be successfully negotiated and ratified, and that the Trans-Pacific Partnership (TPP) be agreed to by its signatory countries.

Ideally, economic growth and rejuvenation of Atlantic trade and investment might also be accompanied by the strengthening of NATO and its component ⑥ military forces, thereby reducing Russia's temptation for predatory behavior toward its neighbors. Such changes might also strengthen the credibility and effectiveness of European and American diplomacy. Or American foreign policy could undergo a shift to make rejuvenation of relations with Europe a priority. Alternatively, a renewed or intensified sense of threat, whether from ⑦ Russia, China, Iran, or from a terrorist movement such as ISIS, could transform public attitudes and provide the political basis and resources for more robust policies and enhanced allied cooperation.

Finally, a different kind of event could stimulate great change. A com-⑧ plete withdrawal and abandonment of Europe by America – though hard to imagine – would create conditions for a harsh test of realist propositions about balancing. In such a case, the Europeans might rehabilitate their militaries in order to counterbalance Russian power. This, however, remains far-fetched, not least because of the nuclear problem and German reticence, as well as the need for deeper European political integration. Indeed, a *sauve-qui-peut* (everyone for himself) response might be more likely.

Hypotheticals such as these are useful in avoiding the temptation simply to extrapolate from existing trends and assumptions. But absent transformational change, the erosion of European and Japanese relative capabilities, and the attrition of the Atlantic relationship place even more weight on America for sustaining world order.

1. Strong, sustained economic recovery
2. Benefit from innovation, technological change
3. Foreign competitors – mired in middle income trap
4. Relaunch of regional & political integration
5. Trade agreements – TTIP & TPP
6. Strengthen NATO
7. Intensified threat from Russia, ISIS, etc.
8. Complete withdrawal from Europe by U.S.

3

Middle East policy

Regional conflicts and threats to national interest

> We have been very clear to the Assad regime, but also to other players on the ground, that a *red line* for us is we start seeing a whole bunch of chemical weapons moving around or being utilized. That would change my calculus. That would change my equation.
>
> – President Barack Obama[1]

Since the end of the Cold War a quarter-century ago, efforts to delineate US grand strategy have been a hardy perennial of writing and debate among foreign policy elites and scholars. The post–Cold War decade, the 9/11 terrorist attacks on New York and Washington, wars in Afghanistan and Iraq, the impact of the financial crisis and great recession, the rise of China, Putin's Russia, and widening upheaval and conflict in the Middle East have given impetus to such efforts. Yet, with the exception of the containment doctrine during the Cold War, achieving a comprehensive grand strategy is probably an unrealistic and unattainable goal. In the absence of a single, unambiguous and overriding threat, the American policy process remains too vast and complex, the chess board of world politics too elaborate, the issue areas too numerous, and the disparity between overall principles and real-world events too great. → needs to have a single, serious threat

For the Obama administration, the president's attempts at setting out a foreign policy concept were initially evident in his Cairo speech and Nobel Peace Prize acceptance address, and subsequently in presidential rhetoric and official statements of national security strategy, though by themselves these served more to describe attitudes, visions, and impulses rather than to create a comprehensive strategy.

---

[1] Italics added. President Barack Obama, speaking on August 20, 2012, quoted in "Obama's Blurry Red Line," *Factcheck.org*, September 6, 2013, www.factcheck.org/2013/09/obamas-blurry-red-line/.

In practice, however, a transformed approach to foreign policy has emerged, and nowhere more so than in US Middle East policies on a wide range of fronts. These have included Iran and its nuclear program, the Syrian conflict, the quest for an Israeli–Palestinian peace, the Arab awakening, disengagement from Iraq and Afghanistan, and responses to the threats posed by al-Qaeda and the Islamic State. Rhetoric and policy have often been at odds in these cases, and actions have at times been inconsistent. Despite a preference for selective disengagement, there has been a marked increase in the use of drone attacks against radical Islamist terrorist groups and their leaders, and the Obama administration has found itself reluctantly drawn back into Iraq as a consequence of the dramatic early successes and territorial conquests by the Islamic State and the near collapse of the Iraqi army. In resuming the bombing in Iraq, Barack Obama became the fourth successive president to commit US forces to action there, following precedents set by George H.W. Bush, Bill Clinton, and George W. Bush.

Regardless of these measures, however, the identifiable pattern is one of disengagement and retrenchment. Initially, President Obama's call to re-emphasize domestic priorities had enjoyed popular backing. The American public had wearied with the passage of time, rising casualties, and the elusiveness of victory, and support for continued troop deployments in Iraq and Afghanistan had eroded. Moreover, foreign policy realist scholars continued to call for a reduction in foreign and military policy commitments abroad, with disengagement from exposed positions in the Middle East, Asia, and Europe, along with a shift to a strategy of offshore balancing.[2]

To some extent the intellectual rationale for retrenchment, especially from the Middle East, also has incorporated ideas of liberal internationalists. Although they do not share the same enthusiasm for pulling back from global engagement, their ideas about the growing importance and robustness of international institutions imply less need for the United States to play a leading role.

Notwithstanding scholarly debates, the Obama administration's Middle East policy, in its preference for disengagement, represents a fundamental shift in American policy and practice. This has been driven by a combination of policymaker beliefs, domestic economic and political constraints, disillusionment with the experiences of intervention in the region, and a desire to shift the policy emphasis elsewhere, as in the "pivot to Asia." Yet rather than provide an effective and durable basis for policy and strategy, are the consequences of this approach likely to be counterproductive in terms of stability, security, and American national interest?

In assessing the question, this chapter begins with a broad description of what the Middle East can be considered to include. It then sets out a basic outline of core US national interests in the region. These provide a benchmark

---

[2] See, e.g., Christopher Layne, "Stuck in the Middle East: Offshore Balancing Is the Right Strategy if Obama Has the Courage for It," *The American Conservative*, (January/February 2016), pp. 24–29.

for comparisons of policy effects over time. Next it summarizes the results of American foreign policy during the half-century after World War II and in the subsequent post-9/11 period. In doing so, it considers regional sources of instability, the unintended consequences of intervention in Iraq, and the impact of the Arab awakening. It then sets out key policy dilemmas and assesses the impact of recent policy shifts on US national interests in the region and concludes that a process of retrenchment and disengagement has contributed to the making of a more dangerous and unstable Middle East.

↳ idea of the book

DEFINING THE MIDDLE EAST

The wider Middle East has been the subject of intense focus since the terrorist attacks of September 11, 2001. However, America has been extensively involved in the region since the end of World War II, and its history there dates back to the late eighteenth century when depredations of the Barbary pirates stimulated the development and expansion of the US Navy and armed intervention along the Mediterranean Coast of North Africa.[3]

The terms "Middle East" and "Near East" can encompass overlapping areas and definitions. A common definition applies to the Arabian Peninsula (Saudi Arabia, Yemen, the Gulf states), Mesopotamia (Iraq, Kuwait, Syria, and parts of Iran and Turkey), the Levant (Syria, Lebanon, Israel, Jordan), and Egypt. A still wider delineation, and the one used here, encompasses the entire Maghreb and extends from the Atlantic Coast of North Africa as far east as Afghanistan and Pakistan. The importance of this more inclusive delineation is that it takes into account not only the twenty-two Arab states and Israel, but also Turkey, Iran, Afghanistan, and Pakistan. It also incorporates an expansive list of the types and sources of conflict. These include struggles between and within states, religions, peoples, ethnicities, tribes, ideologies, and subnational or transnational groups and movements: Arabs, Persians, Turks, Sunnis, Shiites, radical Islamists, Kurds, Alawites, Berbers, Druze, Pashtuns, Muslims, Jews, Christians, and others.

US NATIONAL INTERESTS

As noted above, American involvement in the region dates from the late eighteenth century. Struggles with the Barbary states (largely the coastal regions of present day Morocco, Algeria, Tunisia, and Libya) stemmed from their practice of piracy, ransoming of captives, and demands for protection money. The stark contrast between the ethos of the nascent American republic and that of the local leaders becomes evident in a March 1786 diplomatic exchange reported by John Adams and Thomas Jefferson after a meeting with the Ambassador of Tripoli in

---

[3] For an account of America's role in the early period, see Michael B. Oren, *Power, Faith, and Fantasy: America in the Middle East: 1776 to the Present* (New York: W. W. Norton, 2008).

London in which the latter made demands for protection money as a condition for securing peace:

We took the liberty to make some inquiries concerning the Grounds of their pretentions to make war upon Nations who had done them no Injury, and observed that we considered all mankind as our friends who had done us no wrong, nor had given us any provocation.

The Ambassador answered us that it was founded on the Laws of their Prophet, that it was written in their Koran, that all nations who should not have acknowledged their authority were sinners, that it was their right and duty to make war upon them wherever they could be found, and to make slaves of all they could take as Prisoners, and that every Musselman who should be slain in battle was sure to go to Paradise.[4]

American missionary activity and commerce took place during the nineteenth and twentieth centuries, but it is important to note that – unlike the Ottoman Turks, the British, and the French – the United States was not a Middle East colonial power.

However, US interests in the wider region intensified after the end of World War II and coincided with the steady decline of Imperial Britain. Britain and France, in the 1916 Sykes Picot agreement, had defined the borders of much of Iraq, Syria, Lebanon, Jordan, and the Palestine Mandate, and for much of the intervening period, the British had maintained and enforced order in a stretch of territory from Egypt to the Persian Gulf.

As American national interests in the region evolved and expanded, these came to include four key elements: *first*, the reliable supply of oil to world markets; *second*, preventing the region from falling under the control of a hostile power, which during the Cold War meant the USSR; *third*, support for regional friends and allies; and *fourth*, regional stability. With the British withdrawal from Aden in 1967, the United States took on an increasingly prominent role. Its interests expanded to include counterterrorism and opposition to the proliferation of nuclear weapons. Democracy and human rights also have made an appearance, but this inclusion has been intermittent and mostly more symbolic than substantive.[5]

① oil
② containment
③ Supporting allies
④ Regional stability

[4] American Commissioners to John Jay, March 28, 1786, quoted in Founders Online, National Archives, http://founders.archives.gov/documents/Jefferson/01-09-02-0315.

[5] Barack Obama's own formulations of this list have varied. His September 2013 speech to the UN General Assembly specified four "core interests" in the Middle East for which the United States was "prepared to use all elements of our power, including military force, to secure...." These included defense of allies, the free flow of oil, action against terrorist networks, and halting the spread of WMD. Beyond these core interests, the president also cited peace, prosperity, democracy, human rights, and open markets, but added that these could "rarely" be achieved through unilateral American action. See "Remarks by President Obama in Address to the United Nations General Assembly," September 24, 2013, www.whitehouse.gov/the-press-office/2013/09/24/remarks-president-obama-address-united-nations-general-assembly; Obama's earlier May 19, 2011 State Department speech had included universal rights and described political reform as not "a secondary interest, but support for these principles is a top priority." Quoted in "Obama outlines

An early exercise of the American role took place in February 1945 with the meeting between President Franklin Roosevelt and Saudi King Ibn Saud. The encounter, taking place on board the *USS Quincy* in Egypt's Great Bitter Lake as the president was returning from the Yalta conference, resulted in American commitments to Saudi security and Saudi assurances about the supply of oil. Implementation of these and other vital regional interests was, however, a sometime thing. The twists and turns of policy included a supporting American role in the 1953 coup that ousted Prime Minister Mohammed Mossadegh of Iran. Mossadegh had nationalized the oil industry and political mythology has enshrined the idea of covert, decisive US–British leadership in the coup. In the more than six decades since, American presidents have repeatedly offered apologies to Iran. However, as Ray Takeyh and others have shown, the much touted CIA role was marginal at a time when the mercurial Mossadegh had already lost the support of the merchants, the mullahs, and the military.[6] Moreover, the CIA may have overstated its role at the time in order to enhance its own reputation back in Washington.

THE OLD ORDER AND AMERICAN POLICY IN THE ARAB–ISRAELI CONFLICT

For more than half a century, the existing order in the region as well as the status of most Arab regimes remained remarkably stable – but not peaceful. During the early years of the Cold War, the Eisenhower administration at first sought to embrace the Arab nationalism of Egyptian President Gamal Abdel Nasser by distancing itself from the British and French colonial powers and downplaying support for Israel. During these years, despite President Truman's historic recognition of Israel on May 15, 1948, his administration and then that of President Eisenhower largely turned a cold shoulder to the new Jewish state. They provided no military support and little economic assistance as the Israelis fought to defend themselves against their Arab adversaries and subsequently struggled to absorb 800,000 Jews expelled or fleeing from countries of the Arab Middle East. Indeed, in 1951 the CIA even mounted an illegal covert effort to weaken domestic support for Israel. Kermit Roosevelt, the Agency's top Arabist (and allegedly a leader of the anti-Mossadegh coup), was the driving force behind the creation of a front organization, American Friends of the Middle East. The operation was only revealed in 1967 when the leftist *Ramparts* magazine published information about CIA financial support for domestic US groups.[7]

---

vision of Mideast policy," *UPI News*, May 19, 2011, www.upi.com/Top_News/US/2011/05/19/Obama-outlines-vision-of-Mideast-policy/71621305785255/ph2/, accessed January 13, 2015.

[6] Ray Takeyh, "What Really Happened in Iran: The CIA, the Ouster of Mosaddeq, and the Restoration of the Shah," *Foreign Affairs*, Vol. 93, No. 4, (July/August 2014), pp. 2–12.

[7] Hugh Wilford, *America's Great Game: The CIA's Secret Arabists and the Shaping of the Modern Middle East* (New York: Basic Books, 2014), and see especially the review by Michael Doran, "An Alliance Made of Sand," *Wall Street Journal*, December 12, 2013.

These efforts were, however, largely unavailing. In the early 1950s, Nasser turned to the Soviets for funding of the massive Aswan Dam project and for the supply of arms. Subsequently, in the Suez Crisis of October 1956, the Eisenhower administration not only opposed the Anglo-French reoccupation of the Suez Canal which Nasser had nationalized, but voted with the Soviets in the UN Security Council and put intense political and economic pressure on the British and French to withdraw from the Canal and upon the Israelis to withdraw from the Sinai Peninsula.[8]

During its first two decades, to the extent that Israel enjoyed a special relationship with another country, it was less with the United States than with France. Leaders in Paris and Jerusalem regarded Egyptian President Nasser and his promotion of Arab nationalism as a serious threat. France also provided the original technology for Israel's nascent nuclear program. Though President Charles de Gaulle broke with Israel and tilted toward the Arab states at the time of the June 1967 Six Day War, Israel was armed mostly with French weapons when it achieved its stunning victory.

American policy shifted only gradually, beginning with the July 1958 Middle East crisis.[9] After the pro-Western monarchy of Iraq was overthrown, Israel allowed use of its airspace and provided other support for American and British efforts to stabilize the situation in Jordan and Lebanon. For the administration of President Eisenhower and Secretary of State John Foster Dulles, Israel became a regional asset in the face of increasing Arab nationalism and Soviet pressure.[10]

The relationship grew closer in 1962 with the Kennedy administration's decision to sell Hawk anti-aircraft missiles to Israel in order to counterbalance Soviet arms flowing to Egypt and Syria. This collaboration intensified after the 1967 War and even more so following the Yom Kippur War of October 1973. The provision of arms and foreign aid increased markedly during these years and enjoyed broad public and congressional support. Moreover, during the Cold War decades of the 1960s, 70s, and 80s, Israel proved to be a major source of foreign intelligence and of Soviet weapons, tactics, and military technology captured from USSR's Arab clients.

The Egyptian–Israeli Peace Treaty, signed at the White House in March 1979 exemplified just how important the American role in the Middle East and

[8] E.g., André Beaufre, *The Suez Expedition 1956*, trans. from French by Richard Barry (New York: Praeger, 1969); also Finer, *Dulles Over Suez: The Theory and Practice of his Diplomacy* (Chicago: Quadrangle Books, 1964).

[9] This assessment of US policy toward Israel from the Lebanon crisis of 1958 through the Roadmap agreement of 2002 is adapted from Robert J. Lieber, "Der amerikanische Freund," *Internationale Politik* (Berlin), Vol. 63, No. 5 (May 2008), pp. 68–73 (published in English as, "America and Israel after Sixty Years," in *Democratiya*, Summer 2008), www.democratiya.com/review.asp?reviews_id=171.

[10] See, in particular, the account of this episode by Abraham Ben-Zvi, *Decade of Transition: Eisenhower, Kennedy, and the Origins of the American-Israel Alliance* (New York: Columbia University Press, 1998).

the bond with Israel had become.[11] President Anwar Sadat of Egypt, who had come to office after Nasser's death in 1970, broke with his Russian patron after the October 1973 War and established close ties with the United States. This had the effect of undercutting the Soviet great power presence in the region, and from 1977 onward Washington played a crucial part in helping to bridge Egyptian and Israeli differences. President Jimmy Carter presided over negotiations resulting in the Camp David Accords in September 1978, and with the support of Congress his administration provided large amounts of economic and military aid to Israel and Egypt as a means of insuring implementation of the Peace Treaty. For Israel, this entailed assurances that its security would not be jeopardized and that the costs of relocating bases from the Sinai Peninsula could be offset. For Egypt, there was major economic aid plus reequipping of its armed forces with American weapons and establishment of an important military relationship with the United States.

The close connection between America and Israel meant that only the United States could serve as the indispensable intermediary between the Jewish state and its Arab adversaries.[12] This was not only because of its position as the leading external power in the Middle East, but also because of its credibility and importance to Israel. No other country or international organization was in a position to undertake such a task. Russia, Britain, and France as the former colonial powers, the EU, and the UN could at times play contributory roles, but none possessed the key capacities of the United States.

With the end of the Cold War, the relative strategic importance of Israel for the United States appeared to lessen, but close ties between the two countries persisted. The ongoing centrality of the US role continued to be evident in almost every significant crisis and negotiation. For example, the George H.W. Bush administration's 1990–91 response to Iraq's invasion of Kuwait, culminating in Operation Desert Storm, led to the historic Arab–Israeli Madrid Conference of October 1991. Less than two years later, in September 1993, President Bill Clinton presided over the White House signing of the Declaration of Principles (the Oslo Agreement) between Israel and the Palestinians. During the following year, the Israeli–Jordanian Peace Treaty of October 1994 was based on an agreement reached in Washington three months earlier, and the treaty itself was signed not only by Prime Minister Yitzhak Rabin and King Hussein, but also by President Clinton. Disengagement agreements between Israel and the Palestinian Authority in the mid 1990s involved a key US role,

[11] Lawrence Freedman argues that the Camp David agreement leading to the peace treaty was one of three watershed events in 1978–9, along with the Islamic revolution in Iran and the Soviet invasion of Afghanistan that shaped America's Middle East role. See, *A Choice of Enemies: America Confronts the Middle East* (New York: PublicAffairs, 2008).

[12] The late Saadia Touval made a related point, that because the United States was a "biased intermediary" and a reliable ally of Israel, the Arabs regarded it as better able to win concessions. See *The Peace Brokers: Mediators in the Arab–Israeli Conflict, 1948–1979* (Princeton, NJ: Princeton University Press, 1982).

as did intense though ultimately unsuccessful efforts to broker peace between Israel and Syria and between Israel and the Palestinians in 1999–2000.

After a hiatus marked by the beginning of the second intifada, the coming to office of President George W. Bush, the 9/11 attacks on New York and Washington, and the US-led intervention to oust the Taliban regime in Afghanistan, the Bush administration addressed the Palestinian issue. In a June 24, 2002 speech, the president offered explicit support for the creation of a Palestinian state, while requiring that the Palestinians first abandon terrorism and select new leadership not compromised by corruption, autocracy, and terrorism. In this respect, his words were remarkably explicit:

I call on the Palestinian people to elect new leaders, leaders not compromised by terror. I call upon them to build a practicing democracy based on tolerance and liberty...

And when the Palestinian people have new leaders, new institutions and new security arrangements with their neighbors, the United States of America will support the creation of a Palestinian state, whose borders and certain aspects of its sovereignty will be provisional until resolved as part of a final settlement in the Middle East ... The United States will not support the establishment of a Palestinian state until its leaders engage in a sustained fight against the terrorists and dismantle their infrastructure.[13]

The subsequent "Roadmap" for peace, developed in 2003 in coordination with the EU, Russia, and the UN (the Quartet), aimed at relaunching the peace effort and sought to advance a framework for final status negotiations. Both it and the 2007 Annapolis Conference took place largely under American aegis. However, the incipient civil war between the Fatah-led Palestinian Authority on the West Bank and Hamas-dominated Gaza created an enormous obstacle to any genuinely comprehensive final status agreement between Israel and the Palestinians. The Israeli withdrawal from Gaza in 2005, followed by the violent 2007 takeover by Hamas, had created, in effect, two Palestinian entities, one of which (Fatah) officially supported a peaceful two-state solution while the other (Hamas) remained committed to the eradication of Israel. Not surprisingly, despite elaborate American-led efforts in 2008 with the Israeli government of Ehud Olmert and an even more intense diplomatic engagement in 2013–14, involving Secretary of State John Kerry with Prime Minister Netanyahu and Palestinian President Mahmoud Abbas, the goal of Israeli–Palestinian peace remained out of reach.

Armed attacks from Gaza directed at Israel by rockets and missiles as well as kidnapping and terrorist attacks precipitated military interventions by Israel in December 2008–January 2009 (Operation Cast Lead), November 2012 (operation Pillar of Defense), and July–August 2014 (Operation Protective Edge). In each case the United States sought to negotiate an end to the fighting, though local actors, led by Egypt, were often more central to the process.

[13] "President Bush Calls for New Palestinian Leadership," Office of the Press Secretary, The White House, Washington DC, June 24, 2002.

THE OLD ORDER AND AMERICAN POLICY IN
THE WIDER REGION

The Palestinian–Israeli dimension, despite the intense and even obsessive attention it has received, is but one of many conflicts in the region. The long list of other struggles is more extensive and these often have been more deadly and dangerous. One of the earliest was the Arab "Cold War" that pitted Arab nationalist regimes led by Egypt against more traditional and monarchist countries typified by Saudi Arabia. Their intervention (1965–6) during the Yemen Civil War led to extensive fighting and even Egypt's use of poison gas on the battlefield.

Among other conflicts, the emergence of Palestinian guerrilla groups and terrorism precipitated a struggle for power in Jordan (Black September, 1970), in which more than 20,000 Palestinians died as King Hussein crushed the challenge to his reign. The outcome, at least in part, was shaped by Israel's declared willingness to intervene after Syria began to move tank forces across Jordan's northern border as a sign of support for the Palestinians and as a threat to the Jordanian monarchy itself.

The Iranian Revolution in January 1979 led to the ouster of the Shah, who had been a longtime ally and regional proxy for the United States. The subsequent seizure of the US embassy in Tehran and the holding of its fifty-two diplomatic personnel as hostages was an embarrassment to the Carter administration as was its failed April 1980 "Desert One" hostage rescue operation.

The list continues: Lebanon's civil war, which saw the Reagan administration send troops to Beirut in 1982 as part of an effort to restore stability, but which ended disastrously with the April 1983 bombing by Hezbollah of the US embassy and six months later the suicide truck bomb attack on the US Marine Corps barracks that took the lives of 241 Marines.

The most lethal regional conflict during these years was launched by Saddam Hussein, whose forces invaded Iran in September 1980. The ensuing Iran–Iraq War lasted eight years, and caused between 500,000 and one million military and civilian deaths on the two sides.[14] Saddam routinely used poison gas against Iranian troops and even his own Kurdish population at the town of Halabja in March 1988. While the United States was not a direct participant in the conflict, its fear that the Iranian Revolution might spread led it to tilt toward the Iraqis. American intelligence information including satellite data showing troop locations was provided to Baghdad and the United States sent warships into the Persian Gulf to protect oil and commercial shipments. The

---

[14] Figures for total deaths in the Iran–Iraq War vary widely. For example, a Battle Deaths Dataset developed by a group of political scientists estimated over 600,000 deaths, while the dataset of the Correlates of War Project, estimated 500,000 Iraqi and 750,000 Iranian dead. However, officials of the Iranian and Iraqi governments have offered lower numbers. See Charles Kurzman, "Death Tolls of the Iran–Iraq War," http://kurzman.unc.edu/death-tolls-of-the-iran-iraq-war/, accessed January 12, 2015.

US Navy was drawn into clashes with smaller Iranian boats and installations, and in the spring of 1988 a US cruiser accidentally shot down an Iranian passenger plane over the Gulf. Ironically, the incident was one among a number of factors convincing the Khomeini regime that it could not prevail and would need to end the conflict.

While interstate wars in the Middle East have repeatedly taken place, internal armed conflicts have been numerous too and have become more important and more prevalent in recent years. Ongoing conflicts in Syria, Iraq, Libya, Yemen, and Sudan have provided a huge opportunity for terrorist movements, inflicted massive human costs, and disrupted regional stability. Moreover, additional conflicts are readily conceivable.

Earlier examples of these internal conflicts abound. For example, tensions in Syria between the authoritarian Baathist regime of Hafez Assad and the Sunni Muslim Brotherhood came to a climax at the town of Hama in February 1982. There, Assad's security forces put down the threat while leveling the center of the city and killing at least 20,000 men, women, and children. The United States did not have an obvious stake let alone a role in this conflict, but the massacre briefly opened a window into the type of deadly animosities underlying the region's surface stability.

Saddam Hussein's seizure of Kuwait on August 2, 1990 led to the largest US military engagement in the region. Benefitting from the new world order views of Soviet leader Mikhail Gorbachev and his foreign minister Edward Shevardnadze, and backed by UN Security Resolution 678 authorizing the use of force to liberate Kuwait, the administration of George H.W. Bush deployed a half-million American troops along with 250,000 others from more than three dozen countries. In January–February 1991, the multinational "Operation Desert Storm" swiftly defeated Saddam's forces, driving them out of Kuwait after a four-week air war followed by a ground war lasting a mere 100 hours. At its conclusion, the Bush administration chose not to pursue Saddam to Baghdad or to use force to overthrow his regime. Even so, uprisings by Kurds in the North and Shiites in the South eventually resulted in the United States and Britain, in conjunction with UN resolutions, declaring "no-fly" zones to protect those populations from Saddam's forces and left the United States in an ongoing air power commitment, which it conducted from bases in Saudi Arabia and Kuwait. Subsequently, with Saddam still in power and making life difficult for UN arms inspectors the Clinton administration (1993–2001) found itself pursuing a strategy of "dual containment" against both Iraq and Iran.

AMERICA AND THE MIDDLE EAST AFTER 9/11

Though American policies in the Middle East were sometimes inconsistent and included notable reversals, the United States had by and large succeeded in protecting its national interests there. Consider the four main criteria cited previously. First, apart from the Arab oil embargo of 1973–4, the flow of oil had

national interests
changed

not been dangerously disrupted. Second, not only had the United States prevented the region from slipping under the control of a hostile power, but during
the Cold War Soviet influence had even been rolled back or withdrawn from
countries (Egypt, Afghanistan, Iraq, Syria) where it had gained a foothold. To
be sure, the revolution in Iran had removed a major US ally and elevated Iran
as a regional threat, but the influence of Iran was then counterbalanced by
its rivalry with Iraq as well as by the varying combinations of diplomatic,
economic, and military measures employed by Washington. Third, despite the
debacle in Iran, America had mostly succeeded in supporting its allies and
friends (Israel, Egypt, Jordan, Saudi Arabia, the Gulf states, Morocco, and
others). Turkey, a member of NATO, remained a close ally as well, though
after the Islamist (Justice and Development Party) AKP and its leader Recep
Erdogan came to power in 2002, it gradually and then more conspicuously
distanced itself from the United States. Fourth, despite periodic outbursts of
internal or interstate conflict, especially the Yom Kippur War, Iran–Iraq War,
the Soviet–Afghan conflict, and Desert Storm, the overall configuration of the
region seemed more or less stable.

In the meantime, however, counterterrorism and nuclear nonproliferation were becoming more salient on the list of US national interests. In the
post–Cold War decade (1991–2000), and absent the Soviet threat, framing any
kind of overarching grand strategy proved difficult. Though terrorism and proliferation were now subjects of growing concern, neither seemed to constitute
the kind of danger previously presented by Japan and Germany in World War
II or by the USSR during the Cold War and which had served as the focal
points for grand strategies of victory and then of containment.

Stability did not, however, mean the absence of violence and of lesser
threats. In addition to terrorist attacks in Lebanon there were airplane
hijackings, bombings, and suicide attacks. In 1985 there occurred the dramatic hijacking of TWA Flight 847, followed by the Palestinian terrorist
hijacking of the cruise ship *Achille Lauro* and the murder of an elderly
Jewish passenger, and suicide attacks at airports in Rome and Vienna. In
August 1986, Libyan terrorists bombed the La Belle disco in Berlin, killing
two American soldiers and a Turkish civilian and wounding 229 others.
Subsequent major incidents included the bombing of Pan Am Flight 103
over Lockerbie Scotland in December 1988 which killed 189 Americans and
a dozen people on the ground, a February 1993 truck bomb explosion at the
North tower of the World Trade Center in New York that took the lives of
six people and injured more than 1,000, attacks on US military personnel
in Saudi Arabia including the June 1996 bombing of an air force housing
complex at Khobar Towers in Dhahran that killed nineteen Americans, the
August 1998 suicide truck bombings of US embassies in Nairobi and Dar
es Salaam that left more than 290 dead including twelve Americans, and
in October 2000 the terrorist attack on the *USS Cole* at a port in Yemen
in which seventeen navy crewmen died. In response, sporadic retaliation

took place, including an air attack directed against Libyan leader, Muammar Gaddafi, but those responsible were mostly elusive and the counterterror actions had limited effect.

Proliferation of nuclear weapons and of chemical and biological weapons also proved difficult to counter. In the Middle East concerns arose about both Iran and Iraq. Signs of Iran cheating on its obligations under the Nuclear Nonproliferation Treaty (NPT) were already evident in the 1990s. In the case of Iraq, Israel had preemptively destroyed the Osiraq reactor in June 1981, but a decade later, in the aftermath of Desert Storm, inspectors from the International Atomic Energy Agency (IAEA) and UN (UNSCOM) determined that Saddam Hussein possessed a more extensive program than any of the world's major intelligence services had assumed. The evidence included not only three major covert projects seeking to enrich uranium, but also a workable design for a simple gun-type device that could have been employed as a truck bomb or placed in a shipping container. What the Iraqis lacked at the time (spring 1991) was the fissile material to serve as the explosive core of the device.

A decade later, this experience would influence debate about the status of the Iraqi program and judgments about whether it might be on the verge of acquiring a useable nuclear weapon. For much of the 1990s, the Clinton administration sought to contain Saddam, enforcing the UN embargo on oil sales and weapons and seeking to support the embattled UNSCOM inspectors, with whom Saddam played a repetitive game of "cheat and retreat." This time, however, the intelligence failure would prove to be one of serious over- rather than under-estimation. → wrong intelligence = Iraq war

Despite a number of efforts during the 1980s and early 1990s, including the costly intervention by US Marines in Lebanon in 1982–83, the Reagan and George H.W. Bush administrations had not consistently pursued action against the Iranian-backed Shiite terrorist group Hezbollah. In turn, the Clinton administration did not prioritize the capture or killing of al-Qaeda's leader Osama bin Laden, despite his 1996 proclamation of war against America, terrorist attacks against the US embassies in Kenya and Tanzania (1998) and the *USS Cole* in the Yemeni port of Aden (2000), and declaration that for al-Qaeda to obtain nuclear weapons was a sacred duty. Not surprisingly, the terrorist attacks of September 11, 2001 propelled the threats of terrorism and proliferation to the top of the US policy agenda. → Foreign policy had more of a focus

SOURCES OF MIDDLE EAST INSTABILITY

Raging debates about causes of instability marked the post-9/11 period. Some analysts emphasized Israel and the Palestinian problem, others pointed to the American presence in the region, problems of poverty and underdevelopment, or resentment against the West for colonial and neocolonial domination, but none of these interpretations gave sufficient weight to internal causes within

Arab societies and states. Moreover, emphasis on external causes tended to deprive actors of agency and to pay insufficient attention to the autonomous desires, policies, preferences, and world views of local leaders and movements.[15]

The root causes of instability in the Arab Middle East lie in the profound failures of these societies and their leaders to cope with the disruptive effects of modernity and to meet the economic, social, educational, and political needs of their own peoples. The problem was identified in the widely publicized 2002 United Nations Arab Human Development Report, prepared for the UN by a group of Arab economists. Their study concluded that the contemporary Arab world suffered from profound deficits in freedom, the treatment and lack of empowerment of women, and in the societal diffusion of knowledge and information.[16] Such failures can produce frustration, resentment and even rage, which are then projected outward in forms of transference and scapegoating. These take the form of conspiracy theories and virulent denunciation and hatred of the other: the West, America, Christians, Jews, Shiites, Kurds, and others not of one's own nation, ethnicity, tribe, or sect.

The sources of violent radical Islamism are debatable, but those who blame the United States, the West, or Israel, and the "occupation" of Arab lands,[17] fail to take into account the much deeper underlying causes cited earlier. On this issue, a rigorous scholar of terrorism, Assaf Moghadam, effectively refutes the notion that the main cause of suicide terrorism is resistance to "occupation." He stresses, instead, the manner in which terrorism has metastasized into a "globalization of martyrdom."[18] Moghadam argues that such attacks occur most often in countries where there is no "occupation"; that suicide attacks have often been aimed at targets other than the occupier (e.g., against Shiites, Sunnis, or Kurds in Iraq); and that those who do carry out the attacks are often foreign jihadis rather than locals who have been affected by occupation.

The sources of radical jihadism also can be found in the humiliations that parts of the Arab Muslim world have experienced, not only in recent times, but during the past four centuries. The weight of this resentment was evident in the words of the late Osama bin Laden, whose October 2001 video cited eighty

---

[15] I elaborate on these issues in Robert J. Lieber, *Power and Willpower in the American Future: Why the United States is Not Destined to Decline* (New York: Cambridge University Press, 2012), especially pp. 110–112.

[16] United Nations Development Program, Arab Fund for Economic and Social Development, *Arab Human Development Report 2002* (New York, 2002), www.arab-hdr.org/publications/other/ahdr/ahdr2002e.pdf.

[17] For example, the interpretation of Robert Pape, *Dying to Win: The Strategic Logic of Suicide Terrorism* (New York: Random, 2005); and Robert Pape and James K. Feldman, *Cutting the Fuse: The Explosion of Global Suicide Terrorism and How to Stop It* (Chicago, IL: University of Chicago Press, 2010).

[18] Assaf Moghadam, "Suicide Terrorism, Occupation, and the Globalization of Martyrdom: A Critique of Dying to Win," *Studies in Conflict and Terrorism*, Vol. 29, No. 8 (December 2006); and *The Globalization of Martyrdom: Al Qaeda, Salafi Jihad, and the Diffusion of Suicide Attacks* (Baltimore, MD: Johns Hopkins University Press, 2008).

years of "humiliation" and "degradation" at the hands of the West.[19] These references are to the final collapse of the Ottoman Empire in 1922, followed in 1924 by the end of the Muslim caliphate, the spiritual and temporal authority that had endured since the seventh century. The events predated not only significant American involvement in the Middle East, but also refer to a time more than a quarter-century prior to the creation of the state of Israel.

THE UNITED STATES AND IRAQ – UNEXPECTED CONSEQUENCES

The momentous decision of the George W. Bush administration to seek the ouster of Saddam Hussein and to launch Operation Iraqi Freedom on March 19, 2003 is a subject that extends far beyond the confines of this chapter. In essence, however, Bush's decision to roll the iron dice was a product of multiple factors. Among these were the 9/11 attacks, the rapid success of the initial military operation to defeat the Taliban in Afghanistan, the belief that the United States possessed the military capacity to carry out its objective successfully, and the belief that Saddam was seeking to acquire nuclear weapons and that it was preferable to eliminate this threat preemptively. → reasons to invade

Other factors were at work as well. One was the strategic doctrine set out in the September 2002 National Security Strategy (NSS), with its emphasis on preemption in the face of dire threats, American military primacy, a new multilateralism, and promotion of democracy.[20] Another was the sense that twelve years after Operation Desert Storm, containment of Iraq was eroding and could not be sustained indefinitely. → additional reasons

Still another element involved international legality and the UN role. There had been sixteen UN Security Council sanctions resolutions condemning Iraq for its violations concerning weapons inspections, the terms of the Kuwait cease-fire, and existing UN sanctions. In November 2002, the Security Council unanimously passed Resolution 1441, providing Saddam a "final opportunity" to comply with previous disarmament resolutions. It specified that Iraq remained in "material breach" of the cease-fire provisions of Resolution 687 and threatened "serious consequences" for failure to comply. In January 2003, Hans Blix, the then head of the UN's UNMOVIC inspection operation testified that, "Iraq appears not to have come to a genuine acceptance – not even today – of the disarmament, which was demanded of it and which it needs to carry out to win the confidence of the world and to live in peace."[21] According

---

[19] Quoted from the text of bin Laden remarks, "Hypocrisy Rears Its Ugly Head," as broadcast by Al-Jazeera television on October 7, 2001. *Washington Post*, October 8, 2001.

[20] See the initial assessment of the 2002 NSS by John Lewis Gaddis, "A Grand Strategy of Transformation," *Foreign Policy*, No. 133, November/December 2002, pp. 50–57. For elaboration, see Robert J. Lieber, *The American Era: Policy and Strategy for the 21st Century* (New York: Cambridge University Press, 2007), pp. 39–51.

[21] The Security Council, January 27, 2003: An Update on Inspection, Executive Chairman of UNMOVIC, Dr. Hans Blix, www.un.org/Depts/unmovic/Bx27.htm.

to Blix, Iraq had not yet sufficiently answered the remaining questions about its WMD programs nor accounted for key materials.[22] A final, seventeenth resolution that might have formally authorized the use of force proved unattainable due to Russian, Chinese, and French opposition.

In the event, Operation Iraqi Freedom was undertaken by the United States with a coalition of some forty countries, and with the material or at least symbolic support of two-thirds of the member governments of NATO and the EU.[23] The immediate military objectives of the operation were quickly achieved. The political and regional consequences would prove much more daunting. One of these consequences was that despite previous Security Council Resolutions and Saddam's ongoing violation of the UN sanctions, the American-led operation was widely perceived as illegal and a violation of international law. This became the prevailing interpretation in Europe, and the issue of legitimacy soon fed back into American politics. At the time, however, substantial majorities of the Congress (including a majority of Senate Democrats, and nearly 40 percent of House Democrats) had voted in October 2002 to authorize the use of force, and on the eve of the war, nearly two-thirds of the American public supported the operation.[24] In Iraq itself, the inability to establish a stable post-Saddam political order resulted in a growing insurgency against US forces and lethal violence between Iraq's Sunni and Shiite populations. In 2007–08, the American-led military "surge," in close cooperation with Sunni tribes, put down the brutal and extremist forces of al-Qaeda in Iraq. At the end of 2011, United States withdrew, handing off to a democratically elected government under Nuri al-Maliki. Unfortunately, rather than consolidating any kind of stable and effective rule, Maliki turned to repressing his Sunni rivals and to purging the Iraqi Army officer corps of all but his most loyal cronies. The consequences proved disastrous, with the subsequent collapse of much of the army, and the loss of a third of the country to the fanatical forces of ISIS (the Islamic State of Iraq and Syria), now self-declared as the Islamic State.[25] Maliki's resignation in August 2014

---

[22] Blix later wrote, "It was only by the end of May 2003, after the occupation, that I concluded they [the materials] did not exist." Quoted in "The Importance of Inspections," *Proliferation Brief*, Vol. 7, No. 11, July 26, 2004. Carnegie Endowment for International Peace, www .prolioferationnews.org.

[23] The heads of government of eight European countries signed a letter of support written by then Prime Ministers Tony Blair of Britain and Lose Maria Aznar of Spain. In addition, ten countries of the Eastern European Vilnius group signed a similar letter.

[24] "Would you favor or oppose invading Iraq with U.S. ground troops in an attempt to remove Saddam Hussein from power?" Favor 64 percent, Oppose 33 percent, No opinion 3 percent. Source, Gallup Poll, survey date March 14–15, 2003, www.gallup.com/poll/1633/Iraq.aspx, accessed January 12, 2015. Immediately following the start of the war, on March 20, 2003, a Pew poll found 72 percent of the public describing the use of force as the right decision, www.pewresearch.org/2008/03/19/ public-attitudes-toward-the-war-in-iraq-20032008/.

[25] The Islamic State seeks to impose a new Muslim caliphate throughout the Muslim Middle East and ultimately far beyond. Prior to taking the name this violent radical Jihadist group had been called the Islamic State of Iraq and the Levant (ISIL) or the Islamic State of Iraq and Syria, as

[handwritten: ↗ U.S. involvement & decisions = growth of ISIS]

made possible the appointment as prime minister of the more inclusive Iraqi Shiite leader Haider al-Abadi, but great damage had been done.

The other major consequence of US intervention in Iraq, and arguably one of even greater importance, has been Iran's emergence as the dominant regional power. The Iraq–Iran rivalry had created a tenuous balance, but the elimination of Iraq as a major power and the presence of Maliki's Shiite and pro-Iranian regime, altered the regional balance in a profound way. Iran, together with its proxies and protégées (Maliki, Assad in Syria, Hezbollah, the Iranian Revolutionary Guard's Quds Force) has become the leading regional threat to US allies and interests in the Gulf. To a degree Iran is countered by Sunni neighbors, especially Egypt, Saudi Arabia, the United Arab Emirates, and Jordan, though they lack the cohesiveness, strong state institutions, and power projection capacity to effectively balancing Iran on their own. One of America's most basic and long-term Middle East priorities – preventing territorial control by a hostile power – thus has been undermined and constitutes a policy failure of major proportions.

[handwritten: ↳ Middle East policy = Failure]

THE ARAB AWAKENING

For more than half a century, most Arab regimes maintained themselves as *mukhabarat* states. That is, however corrupt and inadequate they were in meeting the wider economic, social, and political needs of their own populations, they were largely effective in holding onto power through their use of their intelligence and security services. In some countries, the exercise of this power was more subtle and velvet gloved. In others (Gaddafi's Libya, Saddam's Iraq, Assad's Syria), it was brutally conducted and with habitual cruelty.

Ironically, in the immediate aftermath of the initially successful US military campaigns in Afghanistan and Iraq, Arab civil societies gained a greater latitude as regimes such as those of Mubarak in Egypt and Assad in Syria, allowed a limited degree of liberalization. They did so not because they had suddenly become convinced of the wisdom of Montesquieu, Mill, or Madison, but because of indications that the Bush administration was now giving greater weight to political freedom.

This too reflected an emerging US priority in the region. The spread of democracy had been one of four key elements in the 2002 National Security Strategy – it had also been an element of the Clinton 1993 strategy of engagement and enlargement – and in the months after the defeat of Saddam, President Bush emphasized the idea. Speaking in November 2003 to the National Endowment for Democracy, he declared:

Sixty years of Western nations excusing and accommodating the lack of freedom in the Middle East did nothing to make us safe, because in the long run stability cannot be

well as the Islamic State of Iraq and al-Sham (ISIS). Al-Sham is the term for a greater Syria extending well beyond that country's current boundaries into parts of Iraq and Lebanon. The movement is also widely known by the pejorative Arabic acronym "Daesh."

purchased at the expense of liberty. As long as the Middle East remains a place where freedom does not flourish, it will remain a place for stagnation, resentment and violence for export.[26]

Evidence that American rhetoric and leadership, backed by military muscle, can be influential could be found in the space provided at the time for opposition politicians in Egypt, and for elections in Iraq, Afghanistan, the West Bank, and Gaza. In the words of a resilient Lebanese political leader, Walid Jumblatt, head of the Druze community, a man accustomed to operating in a dangerous political environment and not known as a friend of the United States, "The Syrian people, the Egyptian people, all say that something is changing. The Berlin Wall has fallen, we can see it."[27] Soon, however, this permissive political climate receded as the United States found itself increasingly mired in the Iraqi and Afghan insurgencies. It had become clear that there would be neither additional armed interventions nor more forceful demands on Arab autocrats to liberalize.

The authoritarian, corrupt and nepotistic Arab regimes, while seemingly stable, were nonetheless brittle. Most lacked the support of their own people, a situation to a certain extent akin to that of Eastern European regimes prior to the withdrawal of Soviet backing. Suddenly, beginning with an incident in Tunisia in December 2010, cracks appeared and the consequences proved dramatic. In the Tunisian case, an obscure street vendor, Mohamed Bouazizi, pushed beyond what he could endure by abusive and corrupt police, set himself on fire. This desperate act caught public attention that exploded with long suppressed anger at abuses of authority by the country's longtime ruler. Within a month, the seemingly iron-fisted ruler, President Zine El Abidine Ben Ali and his family were driven from the country after twenty-three years in power. The protests proved infectious and quickly spread, first to Egypt, then Libya, Syria, Yemen, and Bahrain.

In each case, longtime authoritarian leaders found themselves embattled, though the outcomes varied. Egyptian President Mubarak resigned in the face of mass protests and loss of support from the army, whereas Gaddafi in Libya found himself facing a brutal civil war that lasted half a year until he was hunted down and killed. But Gaddafi had left his country without effective institutions, and in the ensuing months and years, Libya has slipped into chaos. In turn, the Syrian conflict continued with Assad holding onto power, though with much of the country in ruins, some 350,000 dead, many millions as refugees, and extreme radical Islamists increasingly dominant among the rebels. Meanwhile in Yemen, where a longtime ruler was eventually forced from power, a violent struggle for power erupted, with intervention by the Gulf states, Saudi Arabia, and Iran, along with competing Yemeni factions and

[26] Remarks by President George W. Bush at the National Endowment for Democracy's Twentieth Anniversary Event, Washington, DC, November 6, 2003.
[27] Quoted in David Ignatius, "Beirut's Berlin Wall," *Washington Post*, February 23, 2005.

militias, and rising casualties among the civilian population. Finally, in Bahrain, protests by the majority Shiite population were largely suppressed by the security forces of its Sunni monarchy and from the neighboring Gulf Cooperation Council (GCC) countries, but domestic unrest continued.

POLICY DILEMMAS AND CORE NATIONAL INTERESTS

These tumultuous events were largely unpredicted and as they have continued, important parts of the region have become increasingly violent and unstable. Libya remains in upheaval, the deadly civil war in Syria has deeply affected Iraq, and the fate of both countries and even their existence within present borders is in question. Meanwhile, the Islamic State controls wide swaths of territory and millions of people, Lebanon and Jordan are inundated by a refugee tsunami, Egypt under its military ruler President Abdul Fattah al-Sisi faces dire economic problems and violent opposition from jihadists and elements of the Muslim Brotherhood opposition, Yemen is in disarray, and any solution to the Israeli–Palestinian problem remains distant. Moreover, the future of Afghanistan is uncertain, as most American troops withdraw and Afghan forces and a weak central government face the recurgent Taliban threat.

The Iranian nuclear issue has been resolved on an interim basis through the July 2015 Joint Comprehensive Plan of Actions (JCPOA). However, uncertainties abound and even if Iran were to abide by the terms of the agreement, key restrictions on its nuclear program will end after ten to fifteen years. This will leave the Islamic Republic with a modern uranium enrichment capacity and the ability to build a nuclear weapon in less than a year's time. Moreover, restrictions on Iran's imports of conventional weapons will end after five years and on the import of missiles after eight years. Tehran will possess greater resources with which to support its revolutionary and terrorist proxies in the region, and its leaders have given no indication that they plan to curtail these efforts. Indeed, the ritualistic but repeated chants of "Death to America," "Death to Israel" led by Iranian leaders suggest that their intentions have not been moderated by the JCPOA.

In the period since 9/11, American strategy and policy toward the region have undergone a transformation, from the highly activist and interventionist approach of the George W. Bush administration to the widespread disengagement and retrenchment carried out under the Obama presidency. If the former provoked criticism for its expansive role, the latter has generated complaints that America has come to lack credibility with allies and adversaries. Even in the best of circumstances, the intensity and urgency of Middle East regional problems would create policy dilemmas, but in recent circumstances, American policy and strategy have become particularly problematic.

Here, rather than addressing the specific problems in detail, it is more useful to ask how the core national interests of the United States in the broader

Summary of present situation

Middle East have been affected by existing policy and strategy. To do so, consider each of those interests in turn:

1. **Security of oil supplies.** Direct dependence on Middle East oil has fallen significantly as a result of the domestic oil and natural gas renaissance and the dramatic rise in American oil production, but the United States does continue to be integrated within a global oil economy. Though America is much less vulnerable than at any time since the 1973–74 oil shock, energy interdependence remains a reality. Thus the status of Middle East oil production necessarily affects world oil prices and sectors of the economy closely connected with energy. Upheavals in Syria, Libya, and Iraq as well as instability in Nigeria and Venezuela, have affected oil production and exports from those countries, but increased oil production elsewhere, especially in the United States, Canada, and other nonconflict regions, has more than offset those reductions in supply. In addition, oil production in Iran is increasing with implementation of the JCPOA and the lifting of sanctions. Indeed, with world output of oil ample, markets have been oversupplied and prices have at least temporarily plummeted as the Saudis and others compete to maintain market share. This glut is likely to prove at least partly self-reversing, as more costly exploration and development projects are curtailed, but a major disruption would occur if the kind of upheaval experienced in Libya, Syria, and Northern Iraq were to spread to Saudi Arabia.

In sum, despite potential risks, America's national interest in the security of Middle East oil supplies has not been seriously jeopardized.

2. **Preventing territorial control by hostile powers.** Here, the danger to US interests has become significantly greater, affected both by the consequences of the 2003 Iraq War during the Bush presidency and by subsequent policies and events under the Obama administration. Iran, the major state power in the region, and the crucial external supporter of Hezbollah, Syria, Hamas, and Iraq, remains deeply adversarial toward the United States and its allies. Whether or not it fully complies with the JCPOA, Iran is almost certain to achieve the capability to produce such a weapon at a time of its own choosing. This is likely to make it more risk acceptant rather than risk averse in its regional ambitions. In addition, a major threat now comes from the forces of ISIS/Islamic State in Syria and Iraq. The movement does not now (or at least not yet) control the resources of a bona fide state, but it has made inroads elsewhere in parts of the Maghreb, sub-Saharan Africa, and the Afghanistan–Pakistan border areas.

As an added problem, Russia has established military bases in Syria with the aim of deploying air power and advisers to aid the Assad regime. These deployments provide Moscow with a significant presence in the region for the first time since their expulsion from Egypt by Anwar Sadat in 1973.

3. **Support of regional friends and allies.** Here too, the results are negative. Those countries normally allied or linked with the United States have become

increasingly concerned, see themselves as embattled, or even fear abandonment. Jordan has become more and more vulnerable due to a massive influx of refugees from the fighting in Syria and faces potential threats from the Islamic State. Saudi Arabia, Egypt, the UAE, and Israel are distrustful of US policy in the region, particularly Washington's efforts in recent years to find a modus vivendi with the Muslim Brotherhood, which they see as their enemy. They have been uneasy over the administration's emphasis on relations with Qatar and Turkey (both of them key supporters of Hamas and favorable toward the Muslim Brotherhood), as well as by what they consider to be Washington's excessively conciliatory policies toward Iran. US relations with Israel have also become fraught in recent years, with differences over the peace process, settlements, and at one point during the July–August 2014 Gaza conflict, support by the Obama administration for a cease-fire on terms favorable to Hamas.[28] Relations between Washington and Jerusalem became further exacerbated by bitter differences over the Iran nuclear accord as well as by the antagonistic personal relationship between President Obama and Prime Minister Netanyahu.

More broadly, America's traditional friends in the region see the Middle East affected by a bitter and increasingly violent four-way split and fear that Washington fails to grasp the importance of these fracture lines. The four emerging blocs include, first, a status quo group of traditional mostly Sunni (1) friends and allies including Egypt, Saudi Arabia, Jordan, the United Arab Emirates and most Gulf states, Morocco and Tunisia, plus Israel. Second are Shiite Iran, its Iranian Revolutionary Guard Corps (IRGC), various Shiite (2) militias, and Iranian clients including Hezbollah, Syria, Hamas, and increasingly Iraq. Third, there is the Muslim Brotherhood along with its supporters (3) and allies. For a time, this movement in Egypt semed to be on the ascendant after it succeeded in electing Mohammed Morsi as president in 2012. However, Morsi soon over-reached when he issued an edict granting himself unlimited powers. This triggered wide public opposition and a military coup that brought down his regime and led to violent suppression of the Brotherhood. Elsewhere in the region, the leaders of Turkey and Qatar share many of the ideas of the Muslim Brotherhood. Fourth, there are the violent (4) radical Sunni Islamists of al-Qaeda and its multiple affiliates, as well as the still more fanatical and increasingly dangerous Islamic State with which it fights and yet sometimes cooperates.

---

[28] See, for example, Barak Ravid, "Kerry's Latest Cease-fire Plan: What Was He Thinking?" *Ha'aretz*, July 27, 2014. Ravid wrote, "Kerry isn't anti-Israeli; on the contrary, he's a true friend to Israel. But his conduct in recent days over the Gaza cease-fire raises serious doubts over his judgment and perception of regional events," www.haaretz.com/mobile/.premium-1.607332?v=3AB70A 172CE96761671E1E0AC73F54CC, accessed January 13, 2015. Also Lee Smith, "John Kerry Has Hamas' Back: So Who Has Israel's?" *Tablet Magazine*, July 30, 2014, www.tabletmag.com/jewish-news-and-politics/180793/john-kerry-hamas-ceasefire, accessed January 13, 2015.

4. **Maintenance of regional stability.** Much of the region is in severe turmoil. Civil wars in Syria, Iraq, Libya, and Yemen have intensified, and the Israeli–Palestinian conflict appears far from a solution despite the extraordinary amount of time spent by the Obama administration in seeking a peace agreement. There are risks to stability in Egypt, Jordan, Bahrain, and Lebanon, and the future of Afghanistan after US troop drawdowns remains very much in question. In addition, the vast wave of Syrian refugees that has poured into Turkey, Jordan, and Lebanon poses yet another threat to regional order.

5. **Counterterrorism.** Here too the situation is deteriorating. Despite the successful killing of Osama bin Laden, al-Qaeda affiliates have been extending their reach into North Africa, the Sahel region of Africa, Northern Nigeria, and adjacent areas. In addition, the Taliban poses a continuing threat in Afghanistan. Added to this are the successes of hard-line terrorist groups in Syria and Iraq and the threats to the West that they pose, not only in and of themselves, but in the potential return of thousands of jihadist volunteers who hold European and even US passports.

Terrorism experts such as Daniel Byman and Jeremy Shapiro do argue that the returning foreign fighters threat can be exaggerated and point to factors that can to some extent mitigate this risk, but they acknowledge that "almost inevitably there will be some terrorist attacks in Europe or the United States carried out by returnees from Syria or Iraq."[29] The warning has been borne out not only by the subsequent Paris massacre of November 2015, but by repeated incidents in which security services have interrupted terrorist planning for future attacks.

Thus the Yemen-based al-Qaeda in the Arabian Peninsula (AQAP) took credit for the January 2015 *Charlie Hebdo* massacre in Paris, and in the words of the former Secretary of Defense, Chuck Hagel, the Islamic State "has become a 9/11-level threat to the United States."[30] Though domestic public opinion has become more skeptical about the success of counterterrorism policies, majorities of Americans do support the use of force in combating international terrorism. A total of 77 percent favor US airstrikes against terrorist training camps and other facilities, 60 percent agree with the use of US ground troops for that purpose, and 54 percent support keeping some US troops in Afghanistan beyond 2016 for training and counterterrorism.[31]

[29] Daniel Byman and Jeremy Shapiro, "Be Afraid. Be a Little Afraid: The Threat of Terrorism from Foreign Fighters in Syria and Iraq," Washington, DC: Brookings Institution Foreign Policy Paper No. 34, November 2014, pp. 28–29.

[30] Quoted in Kevin Baron, "Airstrikes Not Enough to Defeat ISIL, Hagel Says," *Defense One*, August 21, 2013, www.defenseone.com/threats/2014/08/airstrikes-not-enough-defeat-isil-hagel-says/92153/.

[31] See Dina Smeltz, Ivo Daalder, Karl Friedhoff, and Craig Kafura, *America Divided: Political Partisanship and U.S. Foreign Policy: Results of the 2015 Chicago Council Survey of American*

6. **Nuclear nonproliferation.** With the JCPOA having been signed and then approved by the UN Security Council, the short-term prospect of an Iranian nuclear weapon has receded. Nonetheless, issues of inspection and enforcement will remain sensitive, especially if Iranian infractions are subtle. Reimposition of sanctions for anything less than a blatant Iranian violation would be controversial and other parties to the agreement will be far more reticent than Washington. Ultimately, if Iran were to acquire a nuclear weapon an American president could face an agonizing choice between inaction and the use of force. At the same time, not only might Israel be inclined to launch a preventive strike, but the risk of a wider multinuclear Middle East would grow alarmingly, since Iran's neighbors such as Saudi Arabia, Egypt, and others would have a powerful motivation to go nuclear as well.

7. **Democracy and human rights.** Though only occasionally treated as a US national interest in the Middle East, this objective remains increasingly elusive. With the exception of Tunisia and possibly Morocco, the promise of the post-2011 Arab Spring has failed almost everywhere, and the policy choices – as in Egypt and Bahrain – remain daunting. The Obama administration has de-emphasized and downplayed democratization and human rights, and data from Freedom House and other respected nonpartisan sources show significant deterioration throughout the region.

CONCLUSION: CAUSES AND CONSEQUENCES

To be sure, much that happens in the Middle East cannot be attributed to action or inaction on the part of the United States. Events are often driven by deep internal and regional causes, but the fundamental question remains the extent to which American policies have influenced outcomes there and how US national interests have been affected. → Focus

The Obama administration's approach to the Middle East embodies a significant change in the degree and kind of US regional engagement. The president's June 2009 Cairo speech promising a "new beginning" provided an initial sign of his views. Subsequent policy statements, for example his West Point speech of May 28, 2014, elaborated on themes of retrenchment and withdrawal.[32] Obama's emphasis on ending the two wars he inherited was clearly his focus, but the West Point address and other presidential speeches and statements did set out a nearly dichotomous choice between war (boots on the ground) and inaction.

> Obama's choice

Public Opinion and U.S. Foreign Policy, Chicago Council on Global Affairs, September 2015, p. 26, www.thechicagocouncil.org/sites/default/files/CCGA_PublicSurvey2015.pdf.

[32] Remarks by the President at the United States Military Academy Commencement Ceremony, US Military Academy-West Point, West Point, New York, May 28, 2014, www.whitehouse.gov/the-press-office/2014/05/28/remarks-president-united-states-military-academy-commencement-ceremony.

For example, Obama told the graduating cadets and their families that, "a strategy that involves invading every country that harbors terrorist networks is naïve and unsustainable." He added, "U.S. military action cannot be the only – or even primary – component of our leadership in every instance." But key policy choices, including those that have been advocated by some of his own senior policy officials, are not those of "invading every country" or of "military action" as the "only" or "primary" foreign policy option. Such a dichotomous approach risks devoting insufficient attention to the enormous range of choices and foreign policy tools available to American policymakers, encompassing not only diplomacy, but economic policy, a wide range of incentives and disincentives, political pressure, military assistance, covert action, and other steps well short of committing troops. → *other ways to take action!*

The administration's initial efforts at outreach to Iran, a reset with Russia, the pursuit of closer relations with China, outreach to the Muslim Brotherhood in Egypt, and an extended hand to America's adversaries proved mostly unavailing. A major reason has been that their policies toward the United States were at least as likely to be the product of internal causes such as ideology, regime self-interest, regional dynamics, and path dependence, and thus were unlikely to be transformed by a more accommodating American policy. Instead, the deeply held beliefs of the Ayatollah Khamenei and policy elites in the Islamic Republic of Iran, the history of modern China and the beliefs and priorities of its Communist Party leadership, and the resentments of President Putin at the breakup of the former Soviet Union (which he labeled the "major geopolitical disaster of the century") have provided much more significant drivers of conduct for these countries.

For the United States, the effects of retrenchment in the Middle East have been deeply problematic. Thus US forces were completely removed from Iraq at the end of 2011, but at the cost of being unable to support the Iraqi armed forces or deter the Maliki regime from its self-destructive policies. In Libya, a reluctant intervention under pressure from Britain and France was described as "leading from behind."[33] It proved crucial in the struggle to oust the Gaddafi regime, but rather than seeking to help stabilize and support a post-Gaddafi government, the administration largely washed its hands of Libya. In Syria, despite calling for Assad to step down and declaring "red lines" about the use of chemical weapons, Obama vacillated and then largely abstained from providing meaningful aid to moderate rebels, who have gone on to suffer the brunt of attacks from both Asad and ISIS. More broadly, this pattern of inaction was accompanied by unsupported rhetoric including calls to "rollback the tide of war" and for the "international community" to step up in Syria. But the absence of effective follow-up not only left wider opportunities for the radical extremes, it also fueled a regionwide perception of weakness and

---

[33] Ryan Lizza, "The Consequentialist: How the Arab Spring Remade Obama's Foreign Policy," *New Yorker*, May 2, 2011.

consequence of rhetoric & no action →

uncertainty, leaving the administration with lessened credibility among allies and adversaries. The consequences of retrenchment and disengagement, measured against core national interests in the region, have been a more dangerous and unstable Middle East.

The subject of American Middle East strategy and policy connects to a broader debate among policymakers and academics. This concerns the likely effects on regional and international order of reduced American involvement. Those favoring a pullback have tended to be less troubled at the prospect and less inclined to foresee negative consequences. Among policy elites, especially those who share the views of the Obama administration, a return to domestic priorities has been seen as beneficial. The Obama emphasis on ending two wars mostly concerned the US role with much less focus on the implications for allies and adversaries. His rhetoric emphasized the role of the international community and a belief that it must take on more responsibility for regional and world order problems.

Among academics favoring retrenchment, realists have mostly assumed that regional balances of power would emerge without the United States needing to reengage unless at some future point its national interests were directly threatened. Globalists, in emphasizing international institutions as well as the increasing emergence of shared norms, assumed that these organizations and ideas, along with increasing involvement of the BRICS, could serve to maintain and enhance world order. Other policy and academic figures have instead warned that the consequences of retrenchment would mean a more disorderly, dangerous international environment, one in which problems of collective action became more acute in the absence of America's active engagement. Foreign policy scholars from a variety of perspectives have shared this concern, for example, Stephen Brooks, Aaron Friedberg, Azar Gat, Robert Kagan, Charles Kupchan, John Ikenberry, Michael Mandelbaum, Henry Nau, William Wohlforth, and the late Samuel Huntington.[34]

With the Middle East as a test case, the initial results lend support to the arguments of those who have advocated sustained engagement. Though the United States has not by any means abandoned the region, its reduced role

---

[34] For example, Stephen Brooks, G. John Ikenberry, and William Wohlforth, "Don't Come Home, America: The Case Against Retrenchment," *International Security*, Vol. 37, No. 3 (Winter 2012–2013), pp. 7–51; Aaron Friedberg, "Same Old Story: What the Declinists (and Triumphalists) Miss," *American Interest* (November 2009), pp. 24–34; Azar Gat, "The Return of Authoritarian Great Powers," *Foreign Affairs*, Vol. 86, No. 4 (July/August 2007), pp. 59–69; Samuel H. Huntington, "Why International Primacy Matters," *International Security*, Vol. 17, No. 4 (Spring 1993), pp. 68–83; Robert Kagan, *The World America Made* (New York: Knopf, 2012); Charles A. Kupchan, *No One's World: The West, the Rising Rest, and the Coming Global Turn* (New York: Oxford University Press, 2012); Robert J. Lieber, *Power and Willpower in the American Future: Why the U.S. Is not Destined to Decline* (Cambridge University Press, 2012); Michael Mandelbaum, *The Frugal Superpower: America's Global Leadership in a Cash-Strapped Era* (New York: PublicAffairs, 2010).

consequences of retrenchment & inaction ↗

has coincided with greatly heightened instability and disorder, expanding civil wars, growing territorial control by hostile actors, increased threats of terrorism, mounting refugee problems, weapons proliferation, potential risks to oil production and export, and appalling abuses of human rights.

Of course, any such inventory can provide only a snapshot of regional realities, but based on the cases cited earlier, the evidence strongly reinforces the case for maintaining America's regional and international involvements.

4

BRICS: stakeholders or free-riders?

> This past month may be remembered as the moment the United States lost its role as the underwriter of the global economic system.
>
> – Lawrence Summers, Former Treasury Secretary and economic adviser to President Obama, on China's establishment of the Asian Infrastructure Investment Bank over the objections of the US[1]

In an increasingly globalized world, power has become more diffused. Especially since the start of the twenty-first century, the BRICS (Brazil, Russia, India, China, and South Africa) and others have emerged as significant actors. The appearance of these and other rising powers is not entirely new, but together they represent an increasing presence in economic, cultural, political, and even security terms. At the same time, the relative weight of Europe and Japan has seemed to ebb as these traditional centers of power have experienced economic and demographic stagnation. Political and scholarly observers have tended to greet these changes as heralding a new era in which BRICS would not only become far more influential in world affairs, but would act to reshape, sustain, and promote international institutions and regimes in an increasingly multipolar world. Thus, in writing about the BRICS, a Brazilian scholar argues that rather than playing a disruptive role, they seek to promote the emergence of a rule-based international order and to pressure America and its allies to more consistently adhere to global norms and rules.[2]

But are these assumptions accurate? Are the BRICS increasingly acting as responsible stakeholders, or is the international order becoming more multipolar without becoming more multilateral? I argue in this chapter that, in practice and across a wide range of issue areas, the BRICS have been less rather than more cooperative in sustaining international institutions and international

---

[1] Lawrence Summers, "A Global Wake-up Call for the U.S.?" *Washington Post*, April 5, 2015.
[2] Oliver Stuenkel, *The BRICS and the Future of Global Order* (New York: Lexington Books, 2015).

order, and that in these circumstances, the engagement of the United States is not only essential for reasons of national interest, but that it is vital for sustaining global order.[3] With these considerations in mind, I address here the interplay between the role of the United States and that of BRICS. The question of America's position is central, not only in terms of national interest, but also because the United States has played a unique role as the world's leading provider of public goods.[4] Consequently, a combination of American retrenchment and BRICS abdication would be likely to weaken multilateral institutions and other elements of international order.

DIFFUSION OF POWER

It is commonplace to describe the contemporary world as one that is exceptionally globalized and in which emerging powers play an increasingly prominent role in regional affairs, the global economy, and international institutions. To be sure, globalization and the diffusion of power are greater now than at any time in the past century. These changes have been driven by economic and financial liberalization, the revolutions in communications, transportation, and information technology, and by the existence of institutions and regimes that the United States and its allies did so much to create and develop during the past seven decades. Nonetheless, the diffusion of power itself is not entirely new. The phenomenon was a consequence of the recovery of Europe, the Soviet Union, and Japan from the ravages of World War II. In addition, the winding down of the colonial era saw the emergence of regional powers.[5]

Bipolarity still remained the dominant structural feature of the international system, but the changes were becoming increasingly evident during the 1970s. This phenomenon gained wider notice when, in a January 1972 *Time* magazine "Man of the Year" interview, President Richard Nixon outlined what he saw as the emergence of a five-power world: the United States, the Soviet Union, China, Europe, and Japan.[6] There was a good deal of hyperbole in this assessment, since the United States and USSR remained the dominant military powers, but the idea captured the way in which the number of relevant actors in world economics and politics was enlarging.

---

[3] On the unique importance of the US role, see Robert J. Lieber, *The American Era: Power and Strategy in the 21st Century* (New York: Cambridge University Press, 2005, 2007).

[4] Michael Mandelbaum, *The Case for Goliath* (New York: PublicAffairs, 2005) and *The Frugal Superpower* (New York: PublicAffairs, 2011). Kupchan, *No One's World*, also sees the United States playing a unique role in sustaining international order, but is pessimistic about its ability to continue to do so.

[5] For an early assessment of diffusion of power and the manner in which the presidencies of Richard Nixon, Gerald Ford, Jimmy Carter, and Ronald Reagan sought to adapt foreign policy strategies in response to it, see Kenneth Oye, Robert J. Lieber, and Donald Rothchild (eds.), *Eagle Defiant: U.S. Foreign Policy in the 1980s* (Boston, MA: Little, Brown, 1983).

[6] *Time* magazine, January 3, 1972.

The rise of OPEC and the 1973–4 oil shock were seized upon by some observers as signaling a profound transfer of wealth and power from the rich Northern world to the global South. The reality was different, however. The OPEC countries rode an oil boom, but the non-oil developing countries were the most negatively affected while the major oil importing countries eventually recovered from the inflation and recession triggered by the oil shock. The 1970s witnessed other events that also seemed to presage a weakening of the United States and a developing multipolarity, and by the end of the decade, Soviet ideologues began to speak of a shift in the correlation of forces. American troops had withdrawn from Vietnam without having accomplished their mission and after having suffered 58,000 fatalities. Soviet-supported movements seemed to be on the upsurge in sub-Saharan Africa and Central America, and in December 1979 the Russians invaded Afghanistan. Meanwhile in November 1979, the Carter administration found itself stymied by the Iranian takeover of the US embassy in Tehran, with its fifty-two American diplomatic personnel taken hostage.

Within a decade, however, these seeming shifts in the balance of power proved to be far less significant. It was the Soviet Union, not the United States, that had become overotretched, and the end of the Cold War, together with the collapse of the USSR itself in December, 1991, left the United States as the sole superpower. Indeed, for much of the following decade, the objection was often heard that America was too powerful.

Since that time, much has changed. The 9/11 attacks, American involvement in more than a decade of wars in Iraq and Afghanistan, and the economic rise of China have refocused attention on an increasingly multipower world and one seemingly more globalized and diverse than ever before. Two caveats are required however. One is that while significantly more countries, especially regional powers, matter in international affairs, the world is not truly multipolar. For all its problems, as well as the ambiguities of its strategy, foreign policy, and leadership, the United States retains a unique and wide-ranging combination of strengths across almost all the dimensions by which one measures power: economic, military, scientific, technological, demographic, geographic, and cultural.[7] To be sure, there has been some attrition of that power, yet the margin between America and others remains substantial. Only China stands as a potential peer competitor, but for at least the medium term China is not in a position to overtake the United States.

---

[7] I argue this in Lieber, *Power and Willpower in the American Future*, pp. 95–117. For a compelling statement of both the durability of US primacy and its stabilizing effects, see William Wohlforth, "The Stability of a Unipolar World," *International Security*, Vol. 24, No. 1 (Summer 1999), pp. 5–41. A quarter century ago, at a previous time when discourse about American decline was pervasive, Henry R. Nau made a similar point about the robustness of America. See *The Myth of America's Decline: Leading the World Economy into the 1990s* (New York: Oxford University Press, 1990).

A second caveat concerns beliefs about the extent and irreversibility of globalization. Exactly a century ago on the eve of World War I, much of the world seemed to have reached an extraordinary degree of interdependence as measured in trade, investment, travel, culture, and the rapid dissemination of the products and ideas of modernity. Complacency about the expansion and durability of these trends was widespread. The British author, Sir Norman Angell, became rich and famous with a bestselling and widely translated book, *The Great Illusion*, published in 1910, in which he condescendingly explained to his readers why a great war could not occur, or if it did it would have to end quickly because none of the belligerents could afford the cost. This sense of optimism engendered by modernization and globalization also can be found in the confident words of *The Economist* in June 1913, citing "tendencies which are slowly but surely making war between the civilized communities of the world an impossibility."[8]

THE BRICS AND GLOBAL GOVERNANCE

The term BRIC, a now-familiar acronym originated by Jim O'Neill of Goldman Sachs in 2001, initially referred to Brazil, Russia, India and China. In 2011 the grouping was widened in order to incorporate South Africa. Together these countries comprise some 40 percent of the world's population and approximately 20 percent of its GDP (substantially more if GDP is measured in purchasing power parity rather than market exchange rates). Though the BRICS have been meeting annually since 2006, the label itself has come to represent the enhanced importance of large emerging markets and has been increasingly understood to include not just these five countries, but others as well. For example, the G-20 group of economies, whose leaders first formally convened in 2008, included in addition to the original G-7 advanced industrial states and the BRICS; Argentina, Australia, Indonesia, Mexico, Saudi Arabia, South Korea, Turkey, and the EU.[9]

The rise of the BRICS was generally welcomed by liberal internationalist and globalist scholars, who tended to see this phenomenon as foreshadowing a gradual transition in which rising actors, China prominent among them, would play an increasing role in transforming international regimes and institutions in a way that gave them more influence while the leading role of the United States would be progressively reduced.[10] President Barack Obama also expressed the hope that China and others would become responsible stakeholders, as did his predecessor, George W. Bush.

As seen by liberal internationalists, this phenomenon of China and BRICS working with the advanced industrial democracies to revise and strengthen

---

[8] Quoted in "The year before the sky fell in," review of Charles Emmerson, *1913: In Search of the World Before the Great War*, in *The Economist*, June 8, 2013.

[9] The original G-7 included the United States, Canada, Britain, France, Germany, Italy, and Japan.

[10] I elaborate on this in *Power and Willpower in the American Future*, pp. 91–95 and 166.

international institutions and the mechanisms of global governance was a welcome consequence of the way in which developing countries had benefitted from the post-1945 global order. The United States had played the central role in creating and enhancing this order, but that now was in need of adaptation in order better to accommodate the rising powers.

In essence, this logic incorporates a functionalist premise, encompassing not only economic issues but even security needs that can, ostensibly, be best satisfied by enhancing, widening, and deepening institutionalized cooperation across many realms. It also reflects the experience of the European Union as it evolved from its origins in the European Coal and Steel Community six decades earlier. However, the implied analogy breaks down on two grounds. First, the circumstances in Europe were unique. These included American security guarantees and a nuclear umbrella, the Cold War threat from the Soviet Union, shared memory of two catastrophic world wars in one generation, and a significant degree of civilizational commonality. Second, while the BRICS and others have unquestionably made enormous gains through the existing international institutional framework, especially for trade, investment, and technology transfer, there is little actual evidence, especially in the security realm, that they are committed to paying the costs of regime maintenance or to become true "stakeholders" in conformity with the wishful thinking of liberal internationalist and globalist authors. Instead, while benefitting from the existing liberal international order, they are more inclined to act as free-riders.

Equally important, liberal internationalists and others tend to assume that international relations are a positive sum game.[11] Experiences with multilateralism and with regional international institutions are said to encourage cooperation. Transparency, reciprocity, and habits of collaboration are seen as self-reinforcing. In order to achieve their own domestic needs for economic growth, countries not only find these experiences beneficial, but such cooperation spills over across related functions and issue areas. A generation ago, scholars writing and theorizing about regional integration in Western Europe defined this process as one of "spillover." For liberal internationalists and globalists there is at least an implied analogy with that European experience despite the immense differences in geography, history, and path dependence.[12]

---

[11] See especially Robert O. Keohane, *After Hegemony: Cooperation and Discord in the World Political Economy* (Princeton, NJ: Princeton University Press, 1984); John Gerard Ruggie (ed.), *Multilateralism Matters: The Theory and Praxis of an Institutional Form* (New York: Columbia University Press, 1993); Josep M. Colomer, *How Global Institutions Rule the World* (New York: Palgrave Macmillan, 2014).

[12] On regional integration, functional integration, and spillover see Ernst Haas, *The Uniting of Europe: Political, Social and Economic Forces, 1950–1957* (Stanford, CA: Stanford University Press, 1958); and *Beyond the Nation-State: Functionalism and International Organization* (Stanford, CA: Stanford University Press, 1969); also Leon Lindberg and Stuart Scheingold, *Europe's Would-Be Polity* (Englewood Cliffs, NJ: Prentice-Hall, 1970).

That assumption has some basis in the areas of economics and trade, though the mercantilist and predatory behavior of China provides a serious contrary indicator. In the security realm, however, there is little reason for such optimism. Cases in point include nuclear proliferation (North Korea, Iran), tensions in East Asia (China, Japan, Vietnam, South Korea, the Philippines, the East and South China Seas), conflicts in the Middle East (Iran, Syria, Saudi Arabia, Qatar, Egypt, Lebanon, as well as Israel and the Palestinians), and Russia's predatory behavior in Ukraine. Nonetheless there are exceptions. Brazil has been active in UN Peacekeeping. It assigns nearly 2,500 military and police personnel to those missions and has played a leading role in Haiti, where it has commanded the UN's operation since 2004. It also has headed the maritime component of UNIFIL (Lebanon) since 2011. In addition, Turkey has participated actively in NATO-led peacekeeping missions in Bosnia (SFOR), Kosovo (KFOR), and Afghanistan (ISAF and the non-combat Resolute Support Mission, RSM).

Skepticism about the BRICS and the momentum assumed by liberal internationalists has not been scarce.[13] Realist scholars have understandably been critical of the assumptions underlying these approaches as well as of the foreign policy choices they imply. But other scholars too have found increasing reason for criticism. For example, Naazneen Barma, Ely Ratner, and Steven Weber have observed that, "Instead of a gradual trend toward global problem solving punctuated by isolated failures, we have seen over the last several years essentially the opposite: stunningly few instances of international cooperation on significant issues."[14] And Stewart Patrick, an expert on globalization at the Council on Foreign Relations, has cautioned that, "The United States should be under no illusions about the ease of socializing rising nations. Emerging powers may be clamoring for greater global influence, but they often oppose the political and economic ground rules of the inherited Western liberal order, seek to transform existing multilateral arrangements, and shy away from assuming significant global responsibilities."[15] In this regard, Zaki Laidi has argued that despite their own heterogeneity, the BRICS actually share a common objective in opposing Western liberal internationalist narratives that run counter to traditional state sovereignty. Instead, they seek to protect their own prerogatives,

---

[13] See Richard Betts's acerbic critique of Ikenberry's *Liberal Leviathan: The Origins, Crisis, and Transformation of the American World Order* (Princeton, NJ: Princeton University Press, 2011), *The National Interest*, May/June 2011, pp. 85–96.

[14] "The Mythical Liberal Order," *The National Interest*, No. 124 (March–April 2013), pp. 56–67 at p. 56. Similarly, twenty-six international policy institutes found multilateral action sorely lacking on the most critical international threats. See, "In New Report Card, Heads of Global Think Tanks Give Poor Grades to International Efforts to Tackle Pressing Problems," News release, Council on Foreign Relations, May 11, 2015, www.cfr.org/global-governance/new-report-card-heads-global-think-tanks-give-poor-grades-international-efforts-tackle-pressing-problems/p36526.

[15] "Irresponsible Stakeholders? The Difficulty of Integrating Rising Powers," *Foreign Affairs*, Vol. 89, No. 6 (November/December 2010), pp. 44–53.

independence of action, and national autonomy in an increasingly interdependent world.[16]

BRICS AS FREE-RIDERS

Other than where clear and unambiguous self-interest is present, the actual record of BRICS cooperation on a wide range of international collective action problems provides little evidence of positive engagement let alone embracing of a "stakeholder" role.[17] Whether examined by issue or country, the pattern is clearly identifiable. For example, on global climate change, the BRICS played a major part in the debacle at the November–December 2009 Copenhagen conference that had been convened to develop a follow-on to the Kyoto Protocol in the form of a new and binding agreement, and to which the EU countries and the Obama administration were committed.[18] Instead, China, India, and others saw the prospect of limits on carbon emissions as harmful to their economic development. By some accounts, they also sought the annual transfer of as much as $100 billion per year from the rich countries to the developing economies. In Copenhagen, the BRICS met separately, shutting out the European backers of a stronger agreement, and the conference ultimately concluded with only a vague statement of objectives.

China, which has gained attention for the vast scale of its production of solar panels and wind turbines, has mainly done so as an export strategy, where it has created a massive surplus of these products and undercut foreign competitors in overseas markets. Meanwhile, despite China's widely heralded commitments to increase the use of solar and wind power, these sources still contribute only a very small fraction of its total energy use. At the same time, China's primary reliance on coal-fired electricity plants, along with an enormous expansion in its domestic auto fleet, has made that country the world's leading source of greenhouse gases, with total carbon dioxide emissions now twice those of the United States. The effort of the EU to bring a case to the World Trade Organization based on dumping and export subsidies of solar panels resulted in China taking retaliatory measures and launching a series of virulent verbal assaults. In response and to mollify Beijing, the EU adopted a much watered-down measure. Meanwhile, Europe and the United States have been reducing their emissions by

---

[16] Zaki Laidi, "BRICS: Sovereignty Power and Weakness," *International Politics*, 2012, Vol. 49, No. 5, pp. 614–632 at pp. 614–615.

[17] Professor Jorge G. Castaneda, a former foreign minister of Mexico, has written skeptically about the BRICS's role in international institutions and the consequences were they to gain significantly greater authority within these. See, "Not Ready for Prime Time: Why Including Emerging Powers at the Helm Would Hurt Global Governance," *Foreign Affairs*, September/October 2010.

[18] See Thomas Rapp, Christian Schwägerl, and Gerald Traufetter, "The Copenhagen Protocol: How China and India Sabotaged the UN Climate Summit," *Der Spiegel*, May 5, 2010.

a total of 60 million tons per year whereas China's have been increasing annually by 500 million tons.[19]

Only in very recent years, as the environmental consequences within China's major cities have become so dire, has the Communist Party leadership embarked on a sweeping new program aimed at reducing domestic air pollution. A July 2015 pledge by China's Prime Minister Li Keqiang on curbing emissions and reducing his country's carbon intensity was widely welcomed, but the actual commitment was merely that its emissions of carbon dioxide would *stop growing* (sic) by 2030.[20] Not only will this require a long, difficult, and gradual period of change and adaptation, but the entire episode reflects the primacy of domestic priorities in shaping state behavior on collective action problems. Meanwhile, China did sign the much heralded December 2015 "Paris Agreement" on climate change, with its long-term goal of limiting global temperature increases to 1.5 degrees Celsius (2.4 degrees Fahrenheit) above pre-industrial levels. However, the agreement itself remains non-binding and lacks provisions for inspection and enforcement.

Human rights is another important – and troubled – arena. Here too, the BRICS's record is negative. For the most part, they not only have been wary of providing international support on the issue, but not infrequently they have cooperated with leaders and regimes involved in major human rights abuses. For example, thanks to a vestigial anticolonial solidarity, South Africa has been reluctant to apply pressure against the brutal and destructive rule of Zimbabwean President Robert Mugabe. After Mugabe was reelected to the presidency in a rushed and badly conducted election that the beleaguered opposition had protested was rigged, President Jacob Zuma of South Africa made a point of congratulating Mugabe on his victory. In addition, South Africa welcomed a visit by Sudanese President Omar al-Bashir despite his having been indicted by the International Criminal Court on charges of mass rape and genocide in Darfur.[21]

Other examples of such BRIC behavior abound. Brazil, a stable democracy, has nonetheless been unwilling to criticize the Castro dictatorship in Cuba. This was clearly evident in a 2012 visit by Brazilian President Dilma Rousseff to Havana, in which trade was emphasized to the complete exclusion of other topics. In turn, Russia has provided major political and military support for the embattled Assad regime in Syria and agreed to supply advanced anti-aircraft missiles to Iran. India had no hesitation in making timber and energy deals with the then dictatorial and corrupt rulers of Burma. China has a long-established pattern of striking trade and investment deals with oppressive regimes even when these rulers were already the object of international sanctions. Beijing

---

[19] "The East is Grey," *The Economist*, August 10, 2013.
[20] Chris Buckley, "China Offers New Pledge on Curbing Emissions," *International New York Times*, July 1, 2015.
[21] "South Africa's Foreign Policy: Clueless and Immoral," *The Economist*, September 5, 2015.

has maintained profitable energy ventures in Sudan, and until recently had a long-standing relationship with the regime in Burma.

* At the UN, China and Russia have routinely opposed Security Council resolutions aimed at human rights violators, especially countries such as Sudan, Iran, and Syria. For example, in October 2011, China and Russia both vetoed an already weakened UN resolution condemning the Syrian regime's human rights abuses, and the three other BRICS countries (Brazil, India, and South Africa) abstained. And in March 2014, after the widely criticized Russian annexation of Crimea, the other BRICS countries supported Russia by abstaining on a UN General Assembly resolution affirming Ukraine's territorial integrity.

* On nuclear proliferation, both China and Russia have resisted stronger measures against Iran and North Korea. For years, prior to the Iran nuclear agreement of July 2015 (the JCPOA), Brazil and Turkey opposed sanctions on Iran, despite condemnation of Tehran by the International Atomic Energy Agency and a half-dozen sanctions resolutions adopted by the Security Council. India, for its part, took steps to increase its oil imports from Iran at a time when the Islamic Republic was still under international sanctions and deliberately bypassed the financial restrictions meant to hinder payments to Tehran.[22]

* The list goes on. The BRICS have not been supportive of the "Responsibility to Protect," even though the principle gained international legal standing as the result of the unanimously adopted UN Security Council Resolution 1674 of April 2006. And China and Russia routinely ignore a long-standing 1951 UN Convention by returning refugees to countries in which they are likely to be persecuted.

* On trade, China continues to pursue predatory practices across a wide range of sectors, even while benefitting enormously from an open international economic order, especially since its admission to the World Trade Organization in 2001. As an example of lack of reciprocity, while its large banks have been able to mount a major push in opening branches in Europe, its own financial sector at home remains largely closed to foreign banks.[23] China remains a notorious violator in the area of intellectual property. It also has been involved in systematic cyberwar against US companies. Brazil, despite possessing the world's sixth largest economy, has responded to a serious slowing of economic growth and exports by adopting protectionist measures including special tariffs, local preferences, content requirements, and the use of special tax rules. It also blocked a US-supported free trade plan for the Americas.

* To round off the list, most of the BRICS themselves suffer from high levels of corruption. According to an index developed by Transparency International

---

[22] India also sent a large trade delegation to Iran. *New York Times*, February 10, 2012.
[23] Simon Denyer, "Foreign Firms Fear a Nationalist China," *Washington Post*, September 8, 2015.

(with number one being least corrupt), Brazil ranks 69th, followed by India 85th, China 100th, and Russia 136th.[24]

Even when the international community has been capable of achieving collective action, the BRICS have dragged their feet. Consider the passage of UN Security Council Resolution 1973 in March 2011, for the purpose of protecting civilians and creating a no-fly zone in Libya, and which in effect authorized the use of force ("all necessary measures") to enforce the resolution against the forces of Colonel Gaddafi. The resolution was widely praised at the time as an example of humanitarian intervention. In fact, however, it was a very rare instance of Security Council agreement on the use of significant force, and though it passed with the required ten votes, the list of countries abstaining is revealing: Brazil, Russia, India, China, and Germany, that is, the four major BRIC states plus Germany, the largest and most important member of the EU and the one most commonly described as a civilian rather than a military power.

Not only are the BRICS reluctant to cooperate with the international liberal order on global governance issues, but their record of cooperation with each other is also limited. Although they have been meeting as a group annually since 2009, and even established a BRIC bank, the differences among them remain considerably greater than their commonalities and little in the way of tangible achievements has resulted. For example, the bank, known as the New Development Bank, did open in July 2015 with headquarters in Shanghai, but while China had sought to have the funding burden for the new bank split equally among the five BRICS countries, the others preferred that China take on the greater burden. Moreover, differences among the BRICS are at least as important as what unites them. Only three are democratic (Brazil, India, South Africa), while two are authoritarian or semi-authoritarian (China, Russia). Two are geopolitical rivals with unresolved border and territorial disputes (China, India). One is primarily an energy, raw materials, and weapons exporter (Russia). Two (Brazil, South Africa) are showing signs of pushing back against predatory export behavior and foreign influence on the part of China. And all find themselves distracted by significant regional challenges or disputes.

Observing this pattern, Harsh V. Pant of King's College London rejects the characterization of the BRICS by South Africa's Jacob Zuma, who has claimed the BRICS as "a credible and constructive grouping in our quest to forge a new paradigm of global relations and cooperation." Instead, Pant concludes that, "The narrative surrounding the rise of the BRICS is as exaggerated as that of

---

[24] For purposes of comparison, the Scandinavians, New Zealand, and Switzerland rank as the top six. Among the major OECD counters, Canada is 10th, Germany 12th, Britain 14th, Japan 15th, United States 17th, and France 26th. Corruption Perceptions Index 2014, Transparency International, http://issuu.com/transparencyinternational/docs/2014_cpibrochure_en?e=2496456/10375881, accessed September 21, 2015.

the decline of the United States."[25] In turn, a former high-level Brazilian official has offered an earthy observation about the self-serving behavior of the BRICS's largest member, China:

Up until now, China is like a very rich person who goes to the restaurant, asks for a very big table and, when it comes to paying the bill, always goes to the toilet – it doesn't pay.[26]

Not only is cooperation among the BRICS countries limited, but each of them faces serious internal problems. Brazil suffers from low oil prices and falling demand for its commodity exports, especially as a result of China's serious economic slowdown. It is also hurt by corruption scandals involving its massive state oil company, Petrobras, and allegedly involves senior political figures. The Russian economy, which is heavily dependent on earnings from energy exports, has been badly affected by the fall in oil prices as well as by US and European financial sanctions in reaction to Moscow's actions in Ukraine. Moreover, corruption, an unpredictable rule of law, and the capricious actions of the increasingly authoritarian Putin government have deterred foreign investment and harmed the economy. South Africa's potential is hurt by problems of inefficiency, infrastructure, corruption, and growing public debt. India has considerable potential and the brightest prospects among its BRICS colleagues, but this depends on the achievement of major economic reforms and infrastructure improvements. Thus for the five BRICS countries, these problems have prevented them from attaining the kind of economic and political weight that had been predicted for them after they gained recognition as a group in 2001. Indeed, the extent to which they have fallen short is reflected in the irony that Goldman Sachs, the investment bank whose own economist coined the term "BRICS," has closed its money-losing BRIC fund that had invested in those countries, but which had declined 21 percent since peaking in 2010.[27]

IMPLICATIONS OF BRICS DEFECTION

In game theory terms, the BRICS have mostly chosen to "defect" rather than "cooperate" with others. If so, what are the consequences? One of these concerns the future of the existing international trading system. Here, as Edward

[25] Harsh V. Pant, "The BRICS Fallacy," *The Washington Quarterly* (Summer 2013), pp. 91–105, at pp. 91 and 103.
[26] Quoted in Robert Kagan, "The Ambivalent Superpower: America and the World Aren't Getting a Divorce. But They're Thinking about It," *Politico Magazine*, February 27, 2014, www .politico.com/magazine/story/2014/02/united-states-ambivalent-superpower-103860_Page2 .html#.VfrwP3 1edMF.
[27] "Goldman's "Goldman's BRIC Era Ends as Fund Folds After Years of Losses," *BloombergBusiness*, November 8, 2015, www.bloomberg.com/news/articles/2015-11-08/ goldman-s-bric-era-ends-as-fund-closes-after-years-of-losses.

Friedman of the University of Wisconsin has observed, China and the BRICS have been free-riders, taking advantage of the US-led Bretton Woods system, financial globalization, the communications and transportation revolutions, and the new international division of labor (NIDL) to grow much faster than the OECD countries (the industrial democracies of the developed world) and to game the system. As a result, he argues, the liberal win–win international trading bargain from which they have reaped disproportionate benefits is being seriously undermined.

In particular, Friedman points to the way in which Chinese policies have created and deepened global imbalances and crises. China especially, but also Germany and Japan, have created "impossible dilemmas" for the industrialized democracies. They have done so through their industrial policies, misaligned (i.e., undervalued) currencies, and funneling of cheap capital into artificially low-priced industrial exports. These measures have enabled them to run up huge trade and currency surpluses ($3 trillion in the case of China) and have hurt exports and employment in the OECD countries.

China did gain wider recognition for the role of the yuan as an international currency with the IMF's November 2015 decision to include it in the basket of currencies, along with the dollar, euro, Japanese yen, and British pound, which make up its Special Drawing Rights (SDRs). However, as Benjamin J. Cohen observes absorption of China's currency, into the international monetary system could provide a means of adaptation, but the scope and effectiveness remain highly uncertain as contrasted with previous successful internationalization of the Deutschmark, the yen, and the euro. In the case of China, Cohen finds the challenges of internationalization to be formidable, requiring "very demanding conditions" and that, "Contrary to predictions of the Yuan's 'inevitable' rise, success is by no means guaranteed."[28] Moreover, China lacks key features of other financial powers, including freely trading their currencies in world markets, predictable rule of law, well-established property rights, and status as genuine market democracies.

Meanwhile, the OECD countries are left with impossible dilemmas, either to cut the value of their currencies, or to decrease the costs of their own exports by seriously reducing the living standards of their own working population – a policy that risks strengthening domestic extremists and demagogues.[29] Consequently, in the words of Dani Rodrik, "major emerging markets (China especially) can no longer … be allowed to remain free riders." Rodrik adds that, "China was globalization's greatest success story during

---

[28] Benjamin J. Cohen, "Will History Repeat Itself? Lessons for the RMB," Paper prepared for workshop on the internationalization of the RMB, Asian Development bank Institute, Tokyo, August 8, 2013, pp. 2 and 26.

[29] Edward Friedman, "China and the World Economy," review essay in *Education About Asia*, Vol. 18, No. 2 (Fall 2013), pp. 65–66.

the last quarter century ... yet it may prove to be the reason for its downfall during the next."[30]

The implication is that BRICS's free-riding behavior is jeopardizing the system itself. Protectionist pressures are rising among developing and advanced countries that have been absorbing massive Chinese export flows and are increasingly reluctant to see further expansion, let alone the worsening impact on their domestic manufactures and employment. These pressures have been further intensified by the lingering long-term effects of the 2008–09 financial and economic shocks, the uneven pace of recovery, and the increasing resistance to programs of austerity in European countries especially, both because of the effects on employment and because of competing interpretations about the effectiveness of such programs and their policy tradeoffs. As evidence of this resistance to more free trade, the World Trade Alert, an independent trade monitoring initiative, has found an increase in protectionist measures in recent years, especially since the slowdown in global growth became apparent in 2012.[31]

DIFFUSION OF POWER, INTERNATIONAL ORDER, AND THE US ROLE

If power has been diffusing, and if BRICS and other rising powers have by and large been unwilling to play a significant role as stakeholders, and if they have been reluctant to adopt the kinds of reciprocity and to cede some forms of sovereignty to regional or global institutions in the manner of the Europeans, can the existing forms of international order be sustained? What then are the implications for international order in both the economic and security realms?

Here, the earlier arguments of authors such as Charles Kindleberger and Robert Gilpin seem once again relevant in pointing to the historic importance of a liberal great power (Great Britain, the United States) in sustaining an open international economic order.[32] They, as well as scholars who have followed, also argued that the presence of a great power military hegemon tends to diminish conflict by damping down regional conflicts and by reducing the likelihood of arms races and wars. Among the authors who share this argument, Stephen Brooks and William Wohlforth have emphasized the stability of

---

[30] Dani Rodrik, *The Globalization Paradox: Democracy and the Future of the World Economy* (New York: Norton, 2012), pp. 236 and 273, quoted in Friedman, "China and the World Economy," p. 66.

[31] *The Global Trade Disorder: The 16th GTA Report*, Global Trade Alert, p. 1, November 12, 2004, www.globaltradealert.org/16th_GTA_report.

[32] Charles Kindleberger, *The World in Depression: 1929–1939* (Berkeley: University of California Press, 1973); and Robert Gilpin, *War and Change in World Politics* (New York: Cambridge University Press, 1981). Also see Daniel Drezner, "Military Primacy Doesn't Pay (Nearly As Much As You Think)," *International Security*, Vol. 38, No. 1 (Summer 2013), pp. 52–79.

American-led post–Cold War unipolarity.[33] Others, however, especially among academic realists, are skeptical and have taken a much more complacent view about stability of the international order without American leadership.

Debate over the wisdom of an activist US foreign policy, essentially engagement versus offshore balancing, has produced cross-cutting cleavages not only among international relations scholars, but in the policy and political communities. For example, an articulate and compelling argument in favor of deep engagement and against American retrenchment comes from Stephen Brooks, John Ikenberry, and William Wohlforth, even though Brooks and Wohlforth have elsewhere made a compelling argument about the durability of American primacy whereas Ikenberry is identified with a liberal internationalist approach. Whatever their differences, however, they agree about the importance of sustaining US leadership abroad.[34]

Those arguing for retrenchment and a significantly reduced presence in Europe, East Asia, and the Middle East variously argue that this shift is necessary to conserve resources, to reduce the risk of entanglement, and to redirect resources to domestic priorities. For the most part they assert that without the United States, regional actors will balance against threats, but in the event that its own security interests are ultimately endangered, America has the capacity to reengage as needed. Barry Posen, for example, contends that because the United States has "command of the commons" it can afford to adopt this kind of strategy, and Robert Pape makes a related argument.[35] In turn, Daniel Drezner argues that the United States has been "badly misguided" in overrelying on military preponderance and instead needs to focus on policies to "rejuvenate economic growth, accelerate job creation, and promote greater innovation and productivity."[36] For Richard Haass, who is skeptical about the capacities of the international community to cope with global problems, the principal threat comes not from abroad but from within and we thus need to put America's house in order.[37] Others, for example Christopher Layne, are convinced that US decline is already so far advanced that the United States will have no choice but to seriously curtail its international commitments.[38]

---

[33] Stephen G. Brooks and William C. Wohlforth, *World Out of Balance: International Relations and the Challenge of American Primacy* (Princeton, NJ: Princeton University Press, 2008).

[34] Stephen Brooks, G. John Ikenberry, and William Wohlforth, "Don't Come Home, America: The Case against Retrenchment," *International Security*, Vol. 37, No. 3 (Winter 2012–2013), pp. 7–51. For a concise version of their argument, see "Lean Forward: In Defense of American Engagement," *Foreign Affairs*, January/February 2013.

[35] Barry Posen, "Command of the Commons: The Military Foundation of U.S. Hegemony," *International Security*, Vol. 28, No. 1 (Summer 2003), pp. 5–46; and "Pull Back: The Case for a Less Activist Foreign Policy," *Foreign Affairs*, January/February, 2013. Also see Robert Pape, "Empire Falls," *The National Interest*, No. 99 (January–February 2009).

[36] Drezner, "Military Primacy Doesn't Pay," p. 79.

[37] Richard Haass, *Foreign Policy Begins at Home: The Case for Putting America's House in Order* (New York: Basic Books, 2013).

[38] Christopher Layne, "This Time It's Real: The End of Unipolarity and the 'Pax Americana,'" *International Studies Quarterly* (February 2012), pp. 1–11. In the same issue see the compelling

Michael Mandelbaum also sees the United States as having little alternative to making these reductions. He finds this a consequence of the serious financial and economic constraints caused by sharply rising entitlement costs with the retirement of the "baby boom" generation and because of large budget deficits. As a result, the cuts will come from defense and foreign policy because that is where the money is. However, unlike many of the others, and because he assesses the US role as critical in addressing common world problems, Mandelbaum foresees adverse consequences as a result of these cutbacks.[39] About other countries' view of the American role, he concludes, "They will not pay for it; they will continue to criticize it; and they will miss it when it is gone."[40]

Yet the fundamental importance of the United States is evident, especially in light of the two critical occasions in the past half-century when the UN managed to authorize collective action in terms of major use of force. One was the passage of UN Security Council Resolution 678 in November 1990, authorizing member countries to use "all necessary means" if Saddam Hussein failed to withdraw Iraqi forces from Kuwait within forty-five days. The other was the March 2011 Resolution 1973 on Libya (cited earlier). However, the 1990 resolution came at the very end of the Cold War and at a time of maximum (and unique) cooperation between Moscow and Washington, amid aspirations for a new world order. Twenty-one years later, the Libya resolution not only saw the BRICS abstain, but in its aftermath Russia and China became increasingly resentful at the way in which the authorization was, in their view, employed as a license for a war to overthrow Gaddafi.

Two additional limitations emerged from the Libya case. First, the French, British, and a half-dozen other European NATO members, who along with key Gulf states (Kuwait, Qatar, and the UAE) took on a conspicuous role while the Obama administration preferred to be "leading from behind,"[41] proved unable to carry this off without strong American involvement. This included not only the initial phase of operations to destroy Gaddafi's air assets, but also the urgent resupply of precision weapons as well as the provision of airborne refueling, intelligence-reconnaissance-surveillance (ISR), and other key coordination tasks. Second, following the fall of the Libyan regime in October 2011, none of the outside powers who had intervened (United States, the Europeans, the Gulf states) were willing to commit sufficient resources to aid the Libyans in restoring order and viable institutions. As a result, a stable political system has yet to emerge from the divergent local groups who took part in the rebellion. Instead, Libya has experienced protracted instability, civil conflict,

critique of Layne by William C. Wohlforth, "How Not to Evaluate Theories," *International Studies Quarterly* (February 2012), pp. 219–222.

[39] Michael Mandelbaum, *The Frugal Superpower* (Washington, DC: PublicAffairs, 2010).
[40] Michael Mandelbaum, *The Case for Goliath* (New York: PublicAffairs, 2005), p. 226.
[41] Ryan Lizza, "The Consequentialist: How the Arab Spring Remade Obama's Foreign Policy," *The New Yorker*, May 2, 2011.

growing jihadist violence, and has become a launching point for refugees. Moreover, rather than the event having served as a wakeup call for European members of NATO to bolster their militaries, these capabilities have mostly continued to erode in the face of economic stringency, aging populations, and declining defense budgets.

DIFFUSION OF POWER AND AMERICAN CAPABILITIES

The assumption that a serious reduction in America's overseas commitments is unavoidable needs to be reexamined. Defense spending reductions were inevitable (as they have been after previous American wars) as the United States ended its major combat role in Iraq and greatly reduced its military forces in Afghanistan. Yet the scale and depth of these cuts, as well as reductions in spending for diplomacy, foreign aid, and other elements of foreign policy were not preordained. The reductions necessitated by the "sequester" were a product of polarized political relationships between the Obama administration and Congress, and were matters of choice rather than necessity. As a result, military forces are being reduced to levels which weaken America's deterrence and defense capabilities.

Although the specific language is seldom used, budget debates, and the arguments among foreign policy scholars cited above, are a variant on "guns versus butter" arguments of long standing. The implication, for example in the writing of Drezner, Haass, Posen, and others, is that America cannot afford both. Indeed, as a society and as a consequence of policy preferences we may not be *willing* to afford both, but in terms of historical precedent and economic burden, the costs of sustaining an active and engaged foreign policy remain well within America's capabilities. Deep cuts in spending for defense and foreign policy, as well as significant reductions in overseas commitments, have everything to do with policy, priorities, politics, and leadership, but are not by themselves an inevitable result of America's material status.

Of course, financial resources are not unlimited, and the United States does face long-term problems of debt, deficits, and the rising costs of entitlement programs. Nonetheless, and despite some erosion in its relative international standing, its material strength and capacity remain unmatched.[42] Authors such as Christopher Layne who see China overtaking the United States typically rely on comparisons of GDP based on purchasing power parity (PPP). Using those figures rather than GDP based on market exchange rates, projections do show China beginning to pull ahead of the United States.[43] However, because

---

[42] I emphasize this in *Power and Willpower in the American Future*, as did Henry R. Nau (cited earlier) in *The Myth of America's Decline*.

[43] In PPP terms, IMF projections show China moving ahead of the United States in 2016. I review earlier GDP data based on both PPP and market exchange rates in *Power and Willpower*, pp. 40–46. The IMF World Economic Outlook Database can be found online at: www.imf.org/external/pubs/ft/weo/2013/01/weodata/index.aspx.

PPP data deal with non-traded goods and services, they significantly overstate the productivity of poor countries and exaggerate the size of their economies.

Both measures have their uses, but as Tim Callen of the IMF Research Department has written, PPP is harder to measure and developing countries get a disproportionately higher weight in calculations when this measure is used rather than market exchange rates.[44] Patrick Honohan of Trinity College, Dublin, makes an even stronger case for market exchange rates, noting that, "PPPs exaggerate the 'size' of poor economies," and adds that their widespread use for this purpose "should be discouraged."[45] Hence the use of GDP data based on market exchange rates rather than PPP remains the preferred indicator for the purposes of international comparison.[46] Using IMF calculations based on market exchange rates, the size of the American economy (22.2 percent of world GDP as of 2016) remains significantly greater than that of China (14.2 percent).

In addition, the absolute size of a country's GDP is not necessarily the most accurate indicator of national power. As Michael Beckley has pointed out, in 1870 China and India possessed the world's largest economies, yet China was being humiliated by Western powers and Japan, while India had become an outright colony of Britain.[47] Instead, GDP per capita is a far better indicator. By that benchmark, the United States will remain far ahead for the foreseeable future, and its lead over China is in the order of 8:1.

Further skepticism about the ineluctable rise of China as well as the other BRICS can be found in the assessment of Simeon Djankov and Antoine Van Agtmael. They identify four fundamental causes that significantly diminish the economic growth of these emerging market countries. First, there is the middle income trap, in which the rapid catch up of past decades is ending, so that growth is leveling off, and it will be more difficult to achieve gains relative to the most developed economies. Indeed, China's economic growth has slowed dramatically, with an accompanying impact on BRICS exporters of energy and raw materials. As a result, commodity prices have dropped and the economies of Brazil, Russia, and South Africa have been contracting.[48] Second, Djankov and Van Agtmael note that the OECD countries actually have been gaining in their competitiveness vis-à-vis the BRICS. The wage gap between emerging

44 Tim Callen reviewed the uses of these two different yardsticks in *Finance and* Development, a quarterly magazine of the IMF. See, "PPP Versus the Market: Which Weight Matters?" *Finance and Development*, Vol. 44, No. 1 (March 2007), www.imf.org/external/pubs/ft/fandd/2007/03/basics.htm.

45 Patrick Honohan, "Stop Misusing PPP Calculations," *Finance and Development*, Vol. 44, No. 3 (September 2007).

46 William Wohlforth notes this in "How Not to Evaluate Theories," cited earlier, pp. 219–222.

47 See Michael Beckley, "China's Century? Why America's Edge Will Endure," *International Security*, Vol. 36, No. 3 (Winter 2011–2012), pp. 41–78.

48 Michael J. Boskin, "The Bloom is Off the BRICS," *Project Syndicate*, June 19, 2015, www.marketwatch.com/story/the-bloom-is-off-the-brics-2015-06-19.

and developed economies has been diminishing, and continuing advancements in technology and manufacturing also yield new advantages for the United States and others. America's energy renaissance also provides it with a major manufacturing cost advantage. Third, increased domestic political uncertainty affects many of the emerging economies, especially as new economic, social, and political demands emerge from increasingly empowered younger populations. Fourth, there is the weakness of domestic institutions among the BRICS and others, affecting social policies, health and pension systems, and environmental policies.[49]

In sum, the contemporary international order has become more diverse, with wider diffusion of power, especially in the economic realm, yet the United States still retains unique capabilities that no other actor possesses. In this world, in which emerging powers are primarily acting as free-riders or even at times as predators (Russia, China), while traditional allies (Europe and Japan) have not been capable of playing greater roles in sustaining international cooperation, America's retrenchment has the effect of weakening international order and adversely affecting its own security.

[49] Simeon Djankov and Antoine Van Agtmael, "BRIC Wall: Is the Golden Age of Emerging Markets Over?" *Foreignpolicy.com*, September 25, 2013.

5

Retreat and its consequences

Since the last National Military Strategy was published in 2011, *global disorder* has significantly increased while some of our comparative military advantage has begun to erode.

> – Gen. Martin Dempsey, Chairman of the Joint Chiefs of Staff[1]

For more than seven decades, the international role of the United States has included, *inter alia*, creating and sustaining international institutions, supporting regional stability, providing deterrence and reassurance for allies, opposing the proliferation of nuclear weapons, underpinning the global economy, promoting trade liberalization and economic development, environmental protection, and – often but not always – encouraging human rights and democratization. In that unique capacity, it effectively served not only as the leader, defender, and promoter of the liberal democracies and market economies, but also of the rules and norms of the existing international order, the durability of which so many take for granted.

Now, however, America is less robustly engaged and faces a world in which power is more diffused. Revisionist states of varying sizes and capabilities – China, Russia, Iran, North Korea, Venezuela – pose more formidable or at least more stubborn challenges to the existing order. At the same time, longtime allies in Europe as well as Japan mostly find themselves less willing or capable of projecting power or of paying significant economic, political, or military costs in addressing common international concerns and sustaining global order. Commitments by countries such as Britain, France, Germany, and other Northern European states to combat climate change or to aid economic development in sub-Saharan Africa represent partial exceptions, as does the French

---

[1] Pentagon Releases National Military Strategy, *Defense News*, July 2, 2015, italics added, www .defensenews.com/story/breaking-news/2015/07/01/pentagon-releases-new-national-military-strategy/29564897/.

role in combating al-Qaeda and ISIS in sub-Sahran Africa (the Sahel), but their overall effect on security and order remains limited.

In addition, neither the BRICS nor other emerging powers have been inclined to contribute to solving collective action problems at the global level, let alone preserving Western inspired rules and institutions toward which their own views range from indifference to hostility. Ironically, that predisposition is typically the case for countries that have greatly benefitted from these arrangements, notably China, but also Brazil, Turkey, Malaysia, and others.

This brings us back to the question of whether or not the active engagement and leadership of a powerful America is essential for the maintenance of regional and world order and for dealing with urgent international problems. A venerable tradition of thinking about foreign affairs argues for the importance of a great power creating and sustaining international order. It draws lessons from the examples of the Persian and Roman Empires in ancient times and in the modern era the roles played by Britain with the *Pax Britannica* of the nineteenth and early twentieth centuries followed by a US-led *Pax Americana* after the end of World War II. As noted in Chapter 4, authors such as Charles Kindleberger and Robert Gilpin emphasized the importance of a liberal great power to provide the hegemonic stability necessary for the successful functioning of an open, prosperous international economic order.[2] A hegemon, even a despotic one, may also reduce military conflict on a regional scale – as in the order imposed and brutally enforced in its periphery by the Soviet Union from 1945 to 1989, and on a smaller scale in Yugoslavia by Marshall Tito and his successors until that country's final breakup in 1992.

The explanation for this phenomenon is that the presence of a great military power tends to discourage geopolitical competition among states within its sphere of influence and thereby make arms races and wars among them less likely.[3] During the first decade of the post–Cold War era, that is the 1990s to the mid 2000s, at a time when the relative power advantage of the United States seemed overwhelming, a number of international relations experts made a compelling case for the stability of a unipolar world.[4] Policymakers, pundits, and scholars who saw American power as relatively stabilizing and benign in its effects often differed on the desirability of specific policies, for example

[2] Charles Kindleberger, *The World in Depression: 1929–1939* (Berkeley: University of California Press, 1973); Robert Gilpin, *War and Change in World Politics* (New York: Cambridge University Press, 1981).

[3] Daniel Drezner makes this argument, as have AFK Organski, George Modelski, William Wohlforth, and others, though Drezner argued that the United States can make deeper cuts in defense expenditure without endangering stability. See Drezner, "Military Primacy Doesn't Pay Nearly As Much As You Think)," *International Security*, Vol. 38, No. 1 (summer 2013), pp. 52–79, at pp. 69, 78–79.

[4] Stephen G. Brooks and William C. Wohlforth emphasized the stability of American-led post–Cold War unipolarity in *World Out of Balance: International Relations and the Challenge of American Primacy* (Princeton, NJ: Princeton University Press, 2008).

intervention in Bosnia and Kosovo in the 1990s, Iraq in 2003, and how to cope with Middle East turmoil, but they tended to favor a robust US foreign policy role and the maintenance of a powerful military capacity.

THE CASE FOR RETRENCHMENT

Others, however, have vigorously disagreed. They tend to be skeptical about foreign intervention, favor offshore balancing, and want to see the United States play a less predominant global role.[5] In broad brush terms and to the extent one can define an Obama Doctrine; it falls into this "realist" category. Indeed, a number of commentators and foreign policy experts have characterized Obama's foreign policy record as that of a "reluctant realist."[6]

Of course, foreign policy doctrines can be difficult to define with precision and are often post-facto definitions provided by observers of a president's rhetoric and conduct. Thus President Harry S. Truman in his March 12, 1947 address to a joint session of Congress calling for aid to Greece and Turkey, did not proclaim, "My fellow Americans, today I am announcing the Truman Doctrine." Nonetheless, the arguments he set out in that historic speech later became identified in precisely those terms.

In contrast, the content of an Obama Doctrine has proved to be elusive. The president himself gave varying responses when directly asked. For example, he told Tom Friedman of the *New York Times*, "The doctrine is: We will engage, but we preserve all our capabilities."[7] On other occasions, Obama seemed to dismiss the need for strategic thinking altogether, asserting, "I don't really even need George Kennan right now,"[8] and describing his approach as "Don't do stupid stuff."[9] Yet members of his national security cabinet did not

[5] A sample of writing by offshore balancers includes, for example, Eric Nordlinger, *Isolationism Reconfigured: American Foreign Policy for a New Century* (Princeton, NJ: Princeton University Press, 1995); Joseph M. Parent and Paul K. MacDonald, "The Wisdom of Retrenchment: America Must Cut Back to Move Forward," *Foreign Affairs*, Vol. 90, No. 6 (November/December, 2011); Stephen M. Walt, "Offshore Balancing: An Idea Whose Time Has Come," *Foreignpolicy.com*, November 2, 2011, http://foreignpolicy.com/2011/11/02/offshore-balancing-an-idea-whose-time-has-come/; Barry Posen, "Pull Back: The Case for a Less Activist Foreign Policy," *Foreign Affairs*, January/February, 2013; and Francis Fukuyama, "Dealing with ISIS," *The American Interest*, March 23, 2015, www.the-american-interest.com/2015/03/23/dealing-with-isis/.

[6] Michael E. O'Hanlon, "President Obama: Reluctant Realist," Brookings Institution, March 16, 2012, www.brookings.edu/blogs/up-front/posts/2012/03/16-obama-ohanlon; John Cassidy, "A Reluctant Realist at West Point," *The New Yorker*, May 28, 2014; Steven R. David, "Obama: The Reluctant Realist," Mideast Security and Policy Studies No. 113, Begin-Sadat Center for Security Studies, Bar-Ilan University, June 7, 2015, http://besacenter.org/mideast-security-and-policy-studies/obama-the-reluctant-realist/.

[7] Thomas L. Friedman, "The Obama Doctrine and Iran," *New York Times*, April 4, 2015.

[8] Quoted in David Remnick, "Going the Distance: On and Off the Road with Barack Obama," *New Yorker*, January 27, 2014.

[9] The phrase was initially cited by Christi Parsons and Paul Richter in "Obama Argues against Use of Force to Solve Global Conflicts," *Los Angeles Times*, April 28, 2014, and was quoted directly

necessarily agree about the lack of need for a strategic vision. Thus, as former Secretary of State Hillary Clinton told the *Atlantic* magazine, "Great nations need organizing principles, and 'Don't do stupid stuff' is not an organizing principle."[10]

As Colin Dueck points out, foreign policy experts have identified the Obama Doctrine's central elements variously, as diplomatic engagement, leading from behind, reliance on drone strikes, a kinder gentler empire, and a lack of genuine strategic thinking.[11] Dueck, a foreign policy scholar at George Mason University, suggests his own definition of the Obama Doctrine and in doing so captures the overall logic of the president's approach as "one of overarching American retrenchment and accommodation internationally, in large part to allow the president to focus on securing liberal policy legacies at home."[12]

The evidence for this assessment can be found both in Obama's policy decisions and in his own words. Notably, in an interview with National Public Radio he framed the choices in foreign policy as not spending "another trillion dollars" in order to deal with ISIS after having done so on "big occupations of foreign countries that didn't turn out that well."[13] He emphasized domestic priorities instead, saying, "we need to spend a trillion dollars rebuilding our schools, our roads, our basic science and research here in the United States; that is going to be a recipe for our long-term security and success."[14]

Obama came to office at a time of powerful reaction against the Iraq War and weariness over the still ongoing Afghan conflict. He had benefitted politically from not having been in the US Senate at the inception of the Iraq campaign, unlike the majority of Democratic Senators (and most Democratic Party presidential aspirants as well as his Republican opponent, John McCain) who had voted in October 2002 to approve the use of force. Initially, there had been solid, even strong public support for both the Afghanistan and Iraq Wars, but by the time of the 2008 election, opinion had shifted and Obama could campaign on ending the wars in Iraq and Afghanistan and on reorienting an American foreign policy that in his view seemed too focused on military power.

Despite Obama's tendency to disavow an overall strategic logic, a set of core assumptions did shape his administration's approach to foreign policy. In this

in Obama's interview with Mark Landler of the *New York Times*, "Obama Warns U.S. Faces Diffuse Terrorism Threats," May 28, 2014. However, it was widely reported that the president in private used saltier language, that is, "Don't do stupid shit." See Mike Allen, "'Don't do stupid sh –' (stuff)," *Politico.com*, June 1, 2014, www.politico.com/story/2014/06/dont-do-stupid-shit-president-obama-white-house-107293.html.

[10] Interview. *The Atlantic*, August 10, 2014.

[11] Colin Dueck, *The Obama Doctrine: American Grand Strategy Today* (New York: Oxford University Press, 2015), p. 1.

[12] *Ibid.*, p. 3.

[13] Transcript: President Obama's Full NPR Interview, December 29, 2014, www.npr.org/2014/12/29/372485968/transcript-president-obamas-full-npr-interview.

[14] *Ibid.*

view, the United States was too powerful, too present, and too provocative in its foreign policy behavior, and these features played a major role in triggering adversarial reactions by other countries. For Obama, these assumptions were accompanied by a deep aversion to putting troops in harm's way and an overriding preference for diplomatic engagement as well as reliance on international institutions, especially the UN.

The "reset" with Russia and extended hand to Iran were examples of that logic. To be sure, the president was no pacifist, and the reliance on Special Forces and drone strikes, the temporary troop surge in Afghanistan, and the killing of bin Laden made that clear. Nonetheless, the impulse toward retrenchment was repeatedly evident, not least when disagreements emerged with more seasoned foreign policy principals in his national security cabinet, for example, Defense Secretaries Robert Gates (2006–11), Leon Panetta (2011–13), Chuck Hagel (2013–15), and Ashton Carter (2015–16) as well as Secretary of State Hillary Clinton. These differences emerged over policies toward Afghanistan, Libya, Syria, and Russia's intervention in Eastern Ukraine.[15] Thus, Gates later described how, in the midst of a contentious White House meeting, he concluded that Obama "doesn't trust his [military] commander ... doesn't believe in his own strategy."[16]

Following his reelection in 2012 Obama prioritized several critical foreign policy objectives, each of which reflected his desire to move away from traditional policy priorities in order to emphasize diplomacy and engagement. These included an opening to Iran based on an agreement to curtail its nuclear program, diplomatic recognition of Cuba, and treatment of global climate change as a national security priority. In his aversion to military intervention abroad, Obama was to some extent following the precepts of realist thinkers, but the emphasis on international institutions also reflected the beliefs of liberal internationalism. That tradition places faith in the stability and centrality of the international order above national priorities and interest. It embodies the notion that those institutions and regimes can effectively represent the consensus and legitimacy of a real-world community and it implicitly favors ceding a degree of national sovereignty to these bodies.

Those beliefs have met the harsh tests of reality. The evidence in recent years, and especially in response to the most urgent, dangerous, and potentially deadly crises, suggests otherwise. This was evident in the weakness or outright failures of the UN, regional bodies, and the international community in Ukraine, Syria, Libya, North Korea, the Congo, and elsewhere.

---

[15] For example, Leon Panetta, *Worthy Fights: A Memoir of Leadership in War and Peace* (New York: Penguin, 2014); Robert Gates, *Duty: Memoirs of a Secretary at War* (New York: Knopf, 2014); Hillary Rodham Clinton, *Hard Choices* (New York: Simon & Schuster, 2014).

[16] Quoted in a Fred Kaplan's review of *Duty*, "Robert Gates' Primal Scream," *Slate.com*, January 14, 2014, www.slate.com/articles/news_and_politics/war_stories/2014/01/robert_gates_duty_the_defense_secretary_s_criticisms_of_obama_and_bush.html.

RETRENCHMENT AS FOREIGN POLICY

Arguably, the two terms of the Obama presidency afford a striking opportunity to test assumptions about American foreign policy and the consequences of decreased global responsibility. It is sobering to examine the results of this approach and the belief that America could instead focus on "nation-building here at home."[17] To do so it is useful to examine several key regional cases.

Russia. A "reset" of relations announced with fanfare in 2009 produced little in the way of tangible achievements. A degree of cooperation did take place on Afghanistan and Iran, and Russia agreed to the "New START" nuclear arms control treaty (which required disproportionate cuts from the US arsenal). However, with the return to the presidency of Vladimir Putin, who replaced Dimitri Medvedev in December 2011, relations quickly deteriorated. Putin adopted an extreme nationalist and revanchist approach toward Russia's neighbors and the West, coupled with a paranoid and conspiratory rhetorical style directed at Europe and especially the United States. Obama did, however, credit Russia as having been "a help" in concluding the July 2015 nuclear deal with Iran.[18]

Only after Russia gave political asylum to Edward Snowden in mid 2013 did the Obama administration finally drop its efforts to improve relations with Moscow.[19] Putin, meanwhile, adopted increasingly demagogic and repressive policies at home and confrontational policies and actions abroad. In February–March 2014, Russian Special Forces in unmarked uniforms (described colloquially as "little green men") intervened to "protect" Russian-speaking civilians in the Crimea region of Ukraine and to seize government facilities. In the following month, in a rigged referendum supposedly producing an 83 percent voter turnout with 97 percent voting in favor, Moscow annexed Crimea to the Russian Federation. Subsequently, Russian forces intervened in Eastern Ukraine, aiding Russian-speaking separatists, first covertly with military personnel in unmarked uniforms and with new but similarly unmarked armored personnel carriers, tanks, and other heavy weapons, and then quite overtly by the spring and summer of 2015.

These actions were widely condemned, but while agreeing to financial sanctions, the Obama administration was reluctant to provide effective defense weapons to Ukraine or even to lead a proactive diplomatic response. Here too, despite Russia's blatant actions and its open violation of international treaties, Obama opposed recommendations for more decisive action from his own current and previous senior military and foreign policy officials as well as from leading Senate Democrats.[20] In order not to provoke Moscow, Obama even

---

[17] Obama repeatedly used the phrase, for example in his address of June 22, 2011 announcing withdrawal of 30,000 troops from Afghanistan; in a weekly address to the nation on May 5, 2012; and in his acceptance speech at the Democratic National Convention on September 6, 2012.

[18] Thomas Friedman, "Obama Makes His Case," *New York Times*, July 15, 2015.

[19] Angela Stent, "The Rain on Russia's Parade," *Project Syndicate*, May 8, 2015.

[20] For example, in late January 2015, eight prominent foreign policy figures, including Michele Flournoy, who served as Deputy Defense Secretary in the first Obama term, and Ivo Daalder,

sidestepped a meeting with NATO Secretary-General, Jens Stoltenberg on his visit to Washington in March 2015.[21] The White House argued that there was no point in providing more powerful weapons to Kiev because Ukraine would still remain unable to defeat Russia in a war.

This argument, which was also aimed at conciliating Moscow and seeking to maintain its cooperation in the Iran nuclear arms negotiations, did not address a much more practical reality. Strengthening the military capabilities of the Ukrainians and enabling them to put up stiffer resistance to the Russians would increase the costs to Moscow of its actions and could very well serve as a disincentive for further escalation. Putin was averse to military casualties and his regime initially denied that Russian soldiers had been killed, even when scores and then hundreds had already died, and the Kremlin attempted to silence Russian mothers who complained about casualties.

President Putin, whose early experiences lay in the former Soviet Union and its KGB intelligence service, would certainly have appreciated the old Leninist maxim, "Probe with a bayonet: if you meet steel, stop. If you meet mush, then push." Thus as long as the human and material costs of Putin's European policies remained relatively modest, there was no reason to stop.

Nor did efforts to avoid provoking Moscow produce changes in Russian behavior. Instead, Putin escalated the rhetoric and policies aimed at NATO and America. As a case in point, Russian forces conducted extensive military maneuvers simulating operations against NATO and especially at the Baltic countries, Poland, and Scandinavia, and involving nuclear-armed submarines, intermediate range nuclear missiles, and strategic bombers.[22] While the United States continued reducing its forces in Europe and drawing down its nuclear arsenal, Russia increased its defense budget and undertook a massive upgrading and modernization of its military. In addition, Moscow has not so subtly threatened its western neighbors and questioned the legality of the Baltic countries' independence at the end of the Cold War.[23]

Obama's former ambassador to NATO, issued a strong statement urging an immediate change in the refusal to supply Ukraine with weapons to defend its besieged eastern provinces. See Daalder, Flournoy, *et al.*, Reserving Ukraine's Independence, Resisting Russian Aggression: What the United States and NATO must Do," Atlantic Council, the Brookings Institution, and the Chicago Council on Global Affairs, February 1, 2015, www.atlanticcouncil.org/publications/reports/preserving-ukraine-s-independence-resisting-russian-aggression-what-the-united-states-and-nato-must-do. Also Jackson Diehl, "Obama's Fight with His Own Party over Foreign Policy," *Washington Post*, February 1, 2015.

[21] Josh Rogin, "Obama Snubs NATO Chief as Crisis Rages," *Bloomberg View*, March 24, 2015, www.bloombergview.com/articles/2015-03-24/obama-snubs-nato-chief-as-crisis-rages.

[22] "Russia Targets NATO with Military Exercises," Stratfor Global Intelligence, *Stratfor.com*, March 19, 2015.

[23] "Russia judiciary questions legality of Baltic countries' independence," *EurActiv.com*, July 1, 2015, www.euractiv.com/sections/europes-east/russian-judiciary-questions-legality-baltic-countries-independence-315906.

Russia under Putin, by its actions in Crimea and Ukraine, has challenged the post–World War II European order and carried out the first change of borders by force there since 1945. Indeed, the then incoming chairman of the Joint Chiefs of Staff, General Joseph F. Dunford Jr., in testimony to Congress, described Russia's aggressive behavior and its nuclear arsenal as the single greatest national security threat facing the United States. He characterized its behavior as "alarming," adding that it "could pose an existential threat."[24]

In sum, policies of engagement and conciliation aimed at Russia have been followed by more aggressive and threatening behavior on its part. To be sure, Russia's conduct is driven by Putin and his thuggish cronies, but America's retrenchment and inaction have played a significant role in shaping the conditions in which this could take place. The consequences have been a more assertive and risk-taking Russia, a much more dangerous and even violent region, and a worsened relationship between Washington and Moscow.

Russia China. Since 2007 Beijing has adopted increasingly hardline policies abroad and stridently nationalist and chauvinist language at home, while discarding its commitment to "peaceful rise" proclaimed at the start of the decade. It has embarked on a sustained, massive modernization of its military, aimed especially at the ability of US air and naval forces to operate in the region. Beijing has claimed territorial waters and small rocky islands in the East and South China Seas far from its own land and that infringe on maritime claims of its neighbors, especially Brunei, Indonesia, Japan, Malaysia, the Philippines, and Vietnam. It has engaged in repeated cyber attacks on the United States, intellectual piracy, theft of corporate and scientific technology, and high-profile cases of espionage. In addition, despite its membership in the World Trade Organization, Beijing has continued to act in a predatory and mercantilist fashion. These actions not only threaten regional peace and stability, but they vitiate a long-held Western and liberal assumption that economic liberalization, trade, membership in international institutions, and the effects of socio-economic modernization would bring about a gradual moderation in China's behavior. → *still time – slow down in economy?*

The threat has not gone unnoticed by leading foreign policy officials. General Dunford's testimony, naming Russia as the number one threat to the United States, cited China second (followed by North Korea and ISIS). In the meantime, the administration's heralded "Pivot to Asia," meant to reassure Asian allies, underpin regional stability, and discourage China from disruptive behavior, was modest in its scope and had limited effect. Perhaps more importantly, reductions in the defense budget and constraints on military manpower and air and naval forces made it difficult to implement a more effective American commitment in the region.

---

[24] Matthew Rosenberg, "Threat of Russian Aggression and Arms Is Singled Out by Joint Chiefs Nominee," *New York Times*, July 10, 2015.

Here too, attributing causality to policies of retrenchment must be approached with some caution. China initially adopted more nationalistic and confrontational policies at the time of the financial crisis in a period that overlapped the end of the Bush administration and the start of Obama's presidency. Nonetheless, arguments that draw a connection are compelling. These go well beyond questions about America's continuing ability to project power in East Asia. China's establishment of the Asian Infrastructure Investment Bank (as discussed in Chapter 2) attracted membership from numerous US allies, despite Washington's efforts to discourage them from joining, and indicates weakening American influence. Statements by foreign elites and journalists reflected the damaging impact of the 2013 "red line" fiasco in Syria on US credibility. Subsequently, the July 2015 Iran nuclear agreement and the perception of trouble between the United States and its longtime Middle East allies fostered skepticism about assurances that America could be relied upon to support Asian allies and maintain its position as leader of a stable regional order.

Iraq and Syria. In retrospect and whatever the plausible case for action at the time, the Bush-led invasion of Iraq in March 2003 with the defeat of Saddam Hussein and dissolution of his Baathist tyranny had disruptive consequences, especially in leaving Iran as the dominant regional power. But whereas Bush has been accused of being too assertive in the use of American power, Obama went to the opposite extreme and those policies have had their own harmful results.

Upon coming to the presidency in January 2009, Obama inherited a relatively stable Iraq. During the previous two years, the "surge" of US troops led by General David Petraeus in close cooperation with the Sunni "awakening" movement had largely succeeded in defeating al-Qaeda in Iraq (AQI). The casualties from terrorist attacks and the lethal conflict between Shiites and Sunnis had been greatly reduced, there was a functioning elected government, a large and increasingly capable American supplied and supported Iraqi Army was in place, and oil production was rising. A drawdown of American forces had begun in the last year of the Bush administration, though 144,000 US troops were still in the country.[25]

The causes of Iraq's near collapse five years later in the face of the ISIS onslaught are disputed, but the manner of American retreat from the country was critical. Obama had committed to the removal of US forces by the end of 2011, but two fateful decisions shaped these events. One concerned the outcome of the 2010 Iraqi elections. Rather than support the creation of a

[25] The troop level is from "Facts and Figures on Drawdown in Iraq," The White House, Office of the Press Secretary, August 2, 2010, www.whitehouse.gov/the-press-office/facts-and-figures-drawdown-iraq. Note that calculations of actual trip numbers vary depending on the methodology used. The number of boots on the ground averaged 158,000 per month in 2008 and 137,000 in 2009. See "Troop Levels in the Afghan and Iraq Wars, FY2001-FY2012: Cost and Other Potential Issues," Amy Belasco, Congressional Research Service, July 2, 2009, http://fas.org/sgp/crs/natsec/R40682.pdf.

government under a multiethnic coalition led by the Shiite but more secular Ayad Allawi, which had won a narrow plurality in the vote, the Obama administration led by Vice President Biden and the then ambassador Christopher Hill supported the Shiite party of the incumbent and Iranian-backed Prime Minister Nouri al-Maliki, who had refused to accept the election results. This choice was made over the strong objections of key US military officials who had been in Iraq, including the commander of US forces there, General Ray Odierno, but was done in the belief it would help speed the end of the war and US withdrawal.[26]

The other fateful event concerned the drawdown of US forces. Military and diplomatic officials had recommended leaving a reduced force of up to 30,000 troops to underwrite stability and provide assistance to the Iraqi military including training, air support, and intelligence.[27] After debates among advisers and disagreements between the White House and the military, the president in June 2011 decided on a figure of 10,000 (later reduced to 5,000). This required renewal of a Status of Forces Agreement (SOFA) to provide legal immunity for US troops, but negotiations to achieve it failed. The reasons for this are contested. According to some accounts, the negotiations might have succeeded if military and economic aid had been better used as leverage, if Obama had not insisted that the SOFA be approved by the Iraqi Parliament, or if the talks had been conducted with greater skill and determination. For example, in July 2015, just prior to his retirement as Army Chief of Staff, General Odierno expressed the view that had the president truly wanted to keep US troops in Iraq, he could have reached a deal to do so.

Others, notably the US ambassador to Iraq from 2010 to 2012, have argued that the political climate in Iraq made an agreement difficult. In the run-up to the US troop withdrawal, the need for their presence appeared less evident and Iraq seemed relatively stable with the security situation much improved. Although most Iraqi political party leaders accepted the need for a US troop presence, immunity for the Americans was unpopular and only 20 percent of the population wanted the troops to remain.[28] Ultimately, in the absence of an agreement, US forces completed their withdrawal in December 2011.

[26] Among numerous accounts, Emma Sky describes General Odierno's bitter disagreement with Ambassador Hill and the White House's decision to support Nouri al-Maliki's continuation ("a Shia strongman") as prime minister. *The Unraveling: High Hopes and Missed Opportunities in Iraq* (New York: PublicAffairs, 2015), pp. 321–322.

[27] General Odierno confirmed that he had recommended keeping 30,000–35,000 troops in Iraq, but the recommendation was not followed. In his view, had the United States stayed "a little more engaged," the rise of ISIS might have been prevented. *Fox News*, July 22, 2015, www .foxnews.com/politics/2015/07/22/exclusive-army-chief-odierno-in-exit-interview-says-us-could-have-prevented/?intcmp=ob_article_footer_mobile&intcmp=obinsite.

[28] "Behind the U.S. Withdrawal from Iraq," James F. Jeffrey, *Wall Street Journal*, November 2, 2014. General Odierno's quote from interview with *Fox News*, July 22, 2015, www .foxnews.com/politics/2015/07/22/exclusive-army-chief-odierno-in-exit-interview-says-us-could-have-prevented/?intcmp=ob_article_footer_mobile&intcmp=obinsite.

In a triumphant address at the Fort Bragg, N.C. Marine base, President Obama proclaimed that with the final departure of the troops, "America's war in Iraq will be over," and "We're leaving behind a sovereign, stable and self-reliant Iraq, with a representative government that was elected by its people. We're building a new partnership between our nations."[29] But Prime Minister Maliki had other ideas. He immediately sought to arrest the Sunni Vice President, Tariq al-Hashimi, who fled to Kurdistan. Maliki then acted to purge Sunni officials and military officers, replacing them with Shiites, many of whom were totally unprepared for these roles or had bribed their way into what they expected to be lucrative positions. Moreover, Maliki repressed and deeply alienated the Sunni population, and violated assurances that the approximately 100,000 tribal fighters of the Sunni Awakening, who had been armed and coordinated by the Americans and played a key role in defeating AQI, would be integrated into the Iraqi Security Forces.

The consequences of these policies proved to be disastrous. In June 2014, Iraq's large, well-armed but abysmally led and demoralized army folded in the face of the ISIS onslaught. Despite greatly outnumbering the attackers, they lost Mosul, the country's second largest city, and large parts of the Sunni heartland in Anbar Province and Northern Iraq. The failures of leadership are vividly illustrated in the lament of an Iraqi soldier after the fall of Mosul, "We were not deserters. Our commanders abandoned us while we were sleeping in the night, and fled by helicopters."[30]

Sunni antagonism toward Maliki and his Shiite regime had become greater than hatred or fear of ISIS. Ironically, ISIS was the linear successor to al-Qaeda in Iraq, which had been largely defeated and expelled from Iraq by US forces in close cooperation with fighters from the Sunni tribes. But with ISIS threatening the stable and relatively successful Kurdish region, slaughtering military and civilian captives and carrying out barbaric crimes against local minorities including the besieged Yazidi population, and with all but a few elite units of the Iraqi Army in a state of disarray or collapse, Obama reluctantly intervened. On June 15, 2014, exactly two and a half years after his triumphant Fort Bragg speech, he announced that a limited number of American forces would be sent to serve as advisers and trainers. In August he ordered the start of airstrikes on ISIS forces in Iraq and Syria, and in September he pledged to "degrade" and ultimately to "destroy" ISIS.

Nonetheless, this renewed commitment in Iraq was modest in contrast to the scale of the problem and size of the country. Within a year the administration had deployed a total of 3,500 troops, but to avoid combat losses or the risk of

---

[29] Remarks by the President and First Lady on the End of the War in Iraq, Fort Bragg, North Carolina, December 14, 2011, The White House, Office of the Press Secretary, www.whitehouse .gov/the-press-office/2011/12/14/remarks-president-and-first-lady-end-war-iraq.

[30] Quoted in the London-based Arab newspaper Ashraq al-Aswat and cited in "Obama's latest Iraq Escalation," *Wall Street Journal*, June 11, 2015.

capture they were largely confined to bases and to training and advisory roles at brigade and division levels, well away from direct contact with the enemy. Nor were they authorized to act as spotters with front line troops to identify targets for airstrikes, thus minimizing the effectiveness of the limited number of attacks being conducted by American aircraft.[31] Ironically, despite these restrictions, by intervening in Iraq, Obama found himself following the path of his recent Oval Office predecessors. In the meantime, as a result of the Iraqi parliamentary elections in April, 2014, Nouri al-Maliki was at last replaced by a more inclusive-minded Shiite successor, Haider al-Abadi. The new prime minister faced an uphill struggle to rebuild the military and regain the support of the Sunni population. However, his weak and embattled government became deeply dependent on Shiite militias and their Iranian sponsors to halt and begin to reverse the advance of ISIS, thus leaving Iran as the dominant force in Iraq. Ironically, it also meant that in the struggle to combat ISIS in Iraq, the United States found itself in an uncomfortable role as a *de facto* partner of Iran.

In retrospect, the American withdrawal from Iraq was pivotal for the resurgence of al-Qaeda in Iraq, now in the form of ISIS. Had the United States not so rapidly disengaged in 2011, a limited but more sustained commitment might well have led to a more stable and effective Iraq, less vulnerable to the onslaught of ISIS, let alone dependence on Iran.

The fate of Syria was also connected to events in Iraq. The rise of ISIS in Syria slowly and then with increasing strength and ferocity over a period of several years provided the base, manpower, and combat experience for its rapid advance into neighboring Iraq. From the outbreak of the Syrian uprising in early 2011, President Obama had been loath to provide serious support for moderate rebels. Though most of his top national security officials favored support for the Free Syrian Army, Obama declined to do so. Even the modest commitments to supplies and training that were made fell short of what was promised, so that more than four years after the outbreak of hostilities, Defense Secretary Ash Carter could testify to Congress that a projected $500 million effort to train and equip thousands of moderate fighters had so far identified only sixty men fit for training.[32] Of these, most were soon captured, killed, or defected, and within two months just four or five of them remained in the field.[33] Obama also opposed

[31] Without spotters and to avoid civilian casualties, nearly 75 percent of US bombing runs targeting the ISIS in Iraq and Syria returned to base without firing any weapons in the first four months of 2015. See, e.g., "U.S. Bombers Hold Fire on Islamic State Targets amid Ground Intel Blackout," *Washington Times,* May 31, 2015, www.washingtontimes.com/news/2015/may/31/us-bombers-hold-fire-on-islamic-state-targets-amid/?page=all.

[32] "Ash Carter's Unwelcome News: Only 60 Syrian Rebels Fit for Training," *Politico,* July 7, 2015, www.politico.com/story/2015/07/ash-carter-syrian-rebel-training-119812.htm. The CIA began covert aid to moderate rebels in 2013, but to become more effective against ISIS and Assad, these rebels later aligned with Jabhat al-Nusra (al Qaeda's Syrian group.) www.thedailybeast.com/articles/2016/01/19/the-cia-s-syria-program-and-the-perils-of-proxies.html.

[33] Testimony to the Senate Armed Services Committee by CENTCOM commander, General Lloyd Austin, September 15, 2015. See "General Austin: Only '4 or 5' US-Trained Syrian

sending arms directly to Iraqi Sunnis or to the Iraqi Kurdish *Peshmerga* forces, who had proved themselves the most effective in fighting ISIS but were at a disadvantage against the Islamic State fighters now armed with more powerful American weapons seized from the Iraqi army. Instead, weapons were channeled through Baghdad, in a slow and inadequate process.[34]

With time, and as the regime of Bashar al-Assad became more and more embattled, the situation in Syria grew increasingly dire. Well over 250,000 people had died and close to half the population had become refugees either outside of Syria's borders or within it. Among the opposition, the moderate Free Syrian Army was increasingly outgunned and outnumbered by the forces of the militant Sunni Islamist groups and by ISIS. In turn the Syrian regime became dependent on Iranian and Shiite fighters from the Revolutionary Guard Corps and from the Iran-backed Lebanese Hezbollah.

As Assad's embattled forces continued to lose ground, Russia intervened, stationing fighter aircraft, surface-to-air missiles, and at least 2,000 military personnel near Syria's Mediterranean port of Latakia to defend the regime's supply lines and its stronghold in the nearby Alawite region.[35] The intervention marked a return of Russian power and influence to the Middle East, a geopolitical shift that American administrations had sought to prevent for seventy years.

In Syria as in Iraq, retrenchment and reluctance to commit American power even indirectly had consequences that threatened US interests and security. The "red line" fiasco reverberated widely beyond the region, calling into question America's reliability and seriousness of purpose. On the ground, the rise of ISIS represented a much greater threat and provided a source of motivation if not direction for terrorist attacks even on America itself. In addition, ISIS spread outside Syria and Iraq, attracting would-be fighters from scores of countries and establishing itself in Afghanistan, Lebanon, Libya, and Nigeria, as well as making forays into Tunisia, the Egyptian Sinai, and elsewhere.

In addition to the threat from ISIS, Iran now had become the leading regional power, with great influence in Iraq, Syria, and Lebanon, as well as with Houthi rebels in Yemen and Hamas in Gaza. And, despite the nuclear agreement, a strengthened Iran (whose ultimate authority Ayatollah Ali Khamenei led chants

---

Rebels Fighting ISIS," *ABC News*, September 16, 2015, http://abcnews.go.com/Politics/general-austin-us-trained-syrian-rebels-fighting-isis/story?id=33802596.

[34] Former Undersecretary of Defense for Policy under Obama, Michele Flournoy, and Richard Fontaine, President of the Center for a New American Security, urged changes in these policies, especially to embed US Special Forces at the battalion level in order to provide advice during military operations, and to furnish forward air controllers who could call in airstrikes to support operations against ISIS. See "To Defeat the Islamic State, the U.S. Will Have to Go Big," *Washington Post, June 24, 2015.*

[35] "Russia to Deploy 2,000 in Syria Air Base Mission's 'first phase'," *Financial Times*, September 21, 2015.

of "Death to America," "Death to Israel") posed a serious threat to Saudi Arabia, the Gulf states, Jordan, and Israel as well as to the US regional role.

"Ratifying Retreat." The Obama foreign policy emphasized diplomacy, dialogue, and engagement, but these are a means not an end in themselves. The results of such diplomatic efforts suggest something altogether different about the signals sent to friends and foes of the United States. Thus, a liberal columnist for the *Washington Post*, Dana Milbank, observing the president's news conference on the conclusion of the Iran nuclear negotiations, focused on the initial failure to secure the release of *Post* reporter Jason Rezaian, one of four Americans held on trumped-up charges in Tehran. In the words of Milbank, not known as a critic of Obama, the president's answers revealed an undercurrent of America's limited power which may amount to "ratifying retreat" and "a powerful case – for American weakness."[36]

A wide range of examples suggests that the Obama approach was almost always based on an overly pessimistic view of America's strength, a consistent preference for retrenchment, and a lack of appreciation for the fact that diplomacy is far more effective when it is backed by power. For example, in the nuclear talks with Iran, Obama and his negotiators signaled their overriding desire to secure a deal. However, the circumstances at the time might have suggested that Iran had the far more urgent need, having seen its oil exports curtailed, its currency value plunge by half, its economy hobbled by stringent sanctions, and its young population increasingly restless. Instead, Obama seemed to court Iran, downplaying its status as a formidable regional foe of the United States, the patron of Hezbollah, the sponsor of terrorism, and responsible for hundreds of American deaths in Iraq, Afghanistan, Lebanon, and the region. Yet, reflecting the administration's effort to minimize Iran's role as an adversary, the annual Worldwide Threat Assessment presented by the Director of National Intelligence, removed both Iran and Hezbollah from its list of terrorism threats.[37] In addition, Obama's own widely quoted words conveyed an unusually accommodating approach, and one that ignored Iran's longtime behavior, when he remarked that Iran could be a "very successful regional power that was also abiding by international norms and international rules."[38]

---

[36] Dan Milbank, "America the Powerless," *Washington Post*, July 16, 2015. Rezaian was released six months later as part of a US–Iranian prisoner swap negotiated separately from the nuclear deal and after the release of Iranian funds that had been frozen as part of the nuclear sanctions against Iran.

[37] In the same document, Iran and seven other countries plus the Islamic State, remained on a longer list of Middle East regional threats. See Statement for the Record, Worldwide Threat Assessment of the US Intelligence Community, Senate Armed Services Committee, James R. Clapper, Director of National Intelligence, February 26, 2015, www.dni.gov/files/documents/Unclassified_2015_ATA_SFR_-_SASC_FINAL.pdf.

[38] Transcript: President Obama's Full NPR Interview, December 29, 2014, www.npr.org/2014/12/29/372485968/transcript-president-obamas-full-npr-interview.

The Iran nuclear deal will remain a major subject of debate as either a crowning achievement of Obama diplomacy or a disastrous folly with potentially catastrophic consequences, but it and the accompanying language with which Iran and the agreement have been described sent a signal, comparable in some respects to the Syria "red line" incident in calling into question America's resolve and steadiness of purpose.[39]

As for Afghanistan, it had been described by Obama during his first campaign for the presidency, as a necessary war. Yet in December 2009, announcing the surge of 30,000 additional troops, Obama dismayed his military commanders by coupling this commitment with a mid-2011 date to begin troop withdrawal. This juxtaposition signaled to the Taliban that they could wait out the offensive and to the local population that it might be prudent not to put too much faith in the resolve and staying power of the Americans.

In the case of Libya, where in March 2011 the UN had approved military intervention, the Obama White House sought to downplay America's role and portrayed itself as "leading from behind." After the fall of Gaddafi in October 2011, the administration largely disengaged and took little part in efforts to stabilize the country. In 2013–14, there was an effort to support the training of a regular Libyan army, but the project floundered amid unrealistic US requirements, lack of coherent institutions and responsible authorities on the Libyan side, and an inability to develop a program that would fit rudimentary needs on the ground.[40] By and large, the United States remained a bystander while Libya slipped into chaos and became a haven for radical Islamist terrorist groups.

Other cases show a similar pattern of retreat and retrenchment. The rapprochement with Cuba and resumption of diplomatic relations was heralded as an historic achievement after fifty-five years of estrangement and antagonism. Yet based on the outcome, the negotiating advantage seemed to have been with the Castro regime, the weaker party, rather than the United States. The agreement offered what the *Washington Post* (which twice endorsed Obama for president) described as a "political and economic bailout of a failing regime."[41] Cuba was taken off the list of state sponsors of terrorism, obtained access to smoother banking transactions, and made significant gains in tourism and trade.

---

[39] Skepticism about Iran has been deep-seated, especially among military leaders. In the words of General David Petraeus, then commander of US forces in Iraq during the "surge," "How does one negotiate with folks like that? They'll pocket what we gave them, bide their time and come back more lethal." Quoted in Emma Sky, *The Unraveling: High Hopes and Missed Opportunities in Iraq* (New York: PublicAffairs, 2015), p. 252.

[40] The failures of a US military training program for Libya are analyzed in Missy Ryan, "Libyan Force Was Lesson in Limits of U.S. Power," *Washington Post*, August 6, 2015.

[41] "Despite Mr. Obama's 'engagement,' Cuba Continues Its Repression," *Washington Post*, July 2, 2015.

For the United States, the deal did remove what had become a long-standing irritant in relations with Latin America and the Caribbean as well as in a number of international forums. Cuba also agreed to improved cooperation on the environment and law enforcement, though in view of its history, its observance of the latter remained to be seen.[42] Moreover, little was achieved on human rights, access by Cubans to information, release of political prisoners, freedom for NGOs to operate, the continuation of ongoing US democracy programs, or even unimpeded access to the local population by American diplomats.[43]

More broadly, the subject of human rights, which had been a shared concern for previous Democratic and Republican presidents, was de-emphasized. The use of human rights language and support for liberty and democracy had been hallmarks of the Carter, Reagan, Clinton, and George W. Bush administrations, and though that commitment was often more symbolic than substantive, it sent a powerful message around the world, serving as an inspiration to those struggling for basic rights as well as a signal about American power and purpose. Now, however, in numerous examples concerning policies toward Russia, China, Iran, Cuba, Venezuela, and others, human rights were largely absent from the agenda, providing an unmistakable signal to repressive regimes about US priorities. The de-emphasis was tangible. US financial support for democracy dropped by some 28 percent during the first six years of the Obama presidency.[44] And while the causal relationship may be indirect, the highly respected Freedom House annual report, *Freedom in the World 2015*, found "More aggressive tactics by authoritarian regimes and … a disturbing decline in global freedom." It described a pattern of almost twice as many countries experiencing declines in human rights as gains, with improvements at their lowest point in nine years.[45]

Then too there was the Obama administration's reticence in naming America's adversaries, the type of caution one might expect of a Finland during the Cold War, reluctant to antagonize the menacing Soviet superpower

---

[42] The Castro regime had at one time or another collaborated with criminal gangs smuggling hard drugs into the United States, provided a haven for foreign guerrillas including Colombians and the Basque ETA, illegally shipped arms to North Korea, and continued to shelter an American fugitive, Joanne Chesimard, convicted in the 1973 killing of a New Jersey state policeman. See an account by Fidel Castro's former bodyguard, Juan Reinaldo Sanchez, *The Double Life of Fidel Castro: My 17 Years as Personal Bodyguard to El Lider Maximo* (New York: St. Martin's Press, 2015).

[43] For a detailed criticism of US policy toward Cuba and the way in which this recognition makes more likely the least favorable model of transition from Communist totalitarianism, see Mike Gonzalez, "The Worst of All Possible Cubas," *The American Interest*, Vol. X, No. 5 (May/June 2015), pp. 33–39.

[44] Tom Carothers, Vice-President, Carnegie Endowment for International Peace, "Why is the United States Shortchanging Its Commitment to Democracy?" *Washington Post*, December 22, 2014.

[45] *Freedom in the World 2015*, Washington, DC, Freedom House, 2015, www.freedomhouse.org/report/freedom-world/freedom-world-2015#.VbFYILXup2A.

on its frontier. Instead, the president's choice of words was almost invariably circumspect when referring to Russia's invasions of Crimea and Ukraine, Iran's support for Hezbollah, or China's intrusions on the maritime rights and resources of its neighbors. Radical Islamist terrorism, even when taking place on American soil, was treated with Orwellian euphemisms. Published reports from the State and Defense Departments as well as the National Intelligence Council referred to "violent extremism" rather than Islamist terrorism. The November 2009 Fort Hood massacre of thirteen unarmed soldiers by Major Nidal Hasan, yelling "allahu akbar" as he continued shooting, was at first labeled "workplace violence." Even the January 2015 killings in Paris drew a muted reaction. On the murder of eleven journalists at the *Charlie Hebdo* newspaper offices, Obama spoke of "cowardly" actions. Two days later, after Islamists deliberately killed four Jews at a Kosher market in Paris, Obama again avoided speaking of Islamic radicalism, instead referring to some "violent, vicious zealots" who "randomly shoot a bunch of folks in a deli in Paris."[46] Further underlining the refusal to name these horrors accurately, neither Obama nor other top US officials joined forty-four heads of state who marched in solidarity with the victims, or in a companion march organized by the French embassy in Washington.

The subsequent November 2015 Paris attack by ISIS also seemed to elicit little empathy, emotion, or forcefulness on the part of Obama. Observers from a wide range of perspectives, including leading Democrats complained of the lack of outrage, and the president was later quoted as telling a meeting of opinion columnists that he did not see enough cable television to fully appreciate public anxiety after the Paris and San Bernardino attacks.[47] The deference toward adversaries was accompanied by a de-emphasis and at times indifference toward allies. Obama was slow to engage with European leaders, prioritizing outreach to adversaries instead, and establishing a personal relationship only with the increasingly autocratic Prime Minister Recep Erdogan of Turkey. This approach contrasted with that of previous presidents, who had coordinated closely with their European counterparts to deal with instability and conflict on Europe's periphery. Thus in the Ukraine crisis, it was largely left to Germany and France to negotiate and seek solutions while Obama remained reluctant to throw America's weight into the negotiations with Russia. Yet not only was this behavior consistent with a pattern of disengagement, but it also worked against administration hopes for the allies to take greater responsibility

[46] Associated Press, "White House Struggles with Obama Comment on Paris Attack," *New York Times*, February 10, 2015.
[47] The Obama off-the-record comment was cited online by Peter Baker, Washington bureau chief for the *New York Times*, and subsequently deleted, in Peter Baker and Gardiner Harris, "Under Fire from G.O.P., Obama Defends Response to Terror Attacks," December 17, 2015. The story and Baker's role was also reported in Erik Wemple, "Peter Baker: Destroyer of a cozy Beltway convention," *Washington Post*, December 17, 2015, and by Noah Rothman, "Obama Cannot Hire His Replacement," Commentary, December 21, 2015.

in addressing wider regional and global problems. As an example, at a time when the French government seemed to favor stronger policies against Russia and Iran, French policy elites warned the leadership to be more cautious in view of Obama's tendency to back down in the face of crises. Far from stepping up, most NATO countries continued to cut their defense spending and reduce troop strength and the capacities of their naval and air forces.

In essence, American policy and strategy had the effect of worsening collective action dilemmas. Regional stability and international order represented a collective benefit or common good, which allies could enjoy whether or not they contributed to securing these. Without clear signs that the United States was substantively committed to engagement and leadership on pressing common problems, Europeans were reluctant to pay the financial and diplomatic costs and more inclined to prioritize their own domestic problems instead. To be sure there were exceptions, as with France's role in the Sahel region of Africa, but these were few and far between.

Middle East allies of the United States also saw themselves as disadvantaged. Saudi Arabia, the Gulf states, and Jordan viewed Iran and its proxies as a great threat and were dismayed by America's reticence, its seeming courtship of Iran, and by Washington's diplomacy which, as in the case of Egypt, seemed to privilege outreach to the Muslim Brotherhood. The fruitless Obama quest for an Israeli–Palestinian peace seemed to many to be a misplaced priority, and backing down over Syria's chemical weapons use resonated far more widely and deeply than was appreciated in Washington. Last but not least, the Obama administration's visible distancing from Israel led Arab leaders to question the dependability of American assurances of support. From their perspective, if the United States could treat such an intimate and longtime friend in this manner, how could they be assured about the credibility of security guarantees to themselves? The author and historian Michael Oren put this bluntly in his memoir about his experience as Israeli ambassador to Washington:

The world, meanwhile, watches us. Friends and adversaries alike – the French and the Iranians, the Japanese, and jihadists – all look at the alliance as a litmus of America's willingness to stand up for its fellow democracy and even to stand up for itself.[48]

RETRENCHMENT AT HOME

Retrenchment is not only a matter of policies abroad, but is closely interwoven with domestic decisions and practices. Obama's approach to foreign policy included an expansive view of international organizations and international cooperation, openings to former adversaries, an end to wars in Afghanistan and Iraq, support for regional peace, and negotiating agreements

---

[48] For a detailed account of the Obama administration's distancing from Israel, see Michael Oren, *Ally: My Journey Across the American-Israeli Divide* (New York: Random House, 2015.) The "litmus" quote can be found at p. 376.

on global climate change, trade, nuclear arms control, nuclear proliferation, and Israeli–Palestinian peace, among other issues. Yet on the domestic front, the steps taken often were inconsistent or undercut these objectives. By reducing America's military capabilities, pulling back from regional and diplomatic commitments, and telegraphing its preference for retrenchment and disengagement, the administration reduced the incentive for allies and others to follow its leadership. Simultaneously, by lessening the likelihood that the United States could or would act to make good on its commitments or threats, it increased the temptation for adversaries to act against American preferences.

Foremost among these domestic constraints was the reduction in the defense budget and in the size and capabilities of the armed forces. In the years after the end of the Cold War, deep cuts had taken place. Defense spending, which had averaged 5.8 percent of GDP in the 1980s, fell to 3.0 percent by the end of the 1990s.[49] The size of the active military force was cut by a third and military commitments abroad were also greatly reduced. For example, in Europe, whereas the United States once stationed some 325,000 troops in 800 installations, by 2015 the number had plummeted to 28,000 in just seven bases. Heavy armor had been pulled out in 2013, three-quarters of military aircraft had been withdrawn, and a US aircraft carrier task force group was no longer stationed in the Mediterranean. Strategic nuclear forces were also radically downsized.[50]

America's spending on defense had risen significantly as a result of the September 11, 2001 attacks and the wars in Afghanistan and Iraq. By 2011 the size of the army had grown to 570,000 troops and the defense budget peaked at 5.1 percent of GDP. With the end of major combat operations in Iraq and the greatly reduced troop numbers in Afghanistan, 80,000 troops were cut from the army in 2012–14 and an additional reduction was announced in July 2015, leaving the army with a projected total of 450,000 by October 2017, its lowest number of active duty troops since 9/11. These figures do not include the additional reductions that would be required were the "sequester" mandated cuts to come into effect. In the words of Joint Chiefs Chairman, General Joseph Dunford, the consequences for US military forces would be "catastrophic."[51]

[49] Data from table 6.1 Composition of Outlays: 1940–2018, "Historical Tables," *Fiscal Year 2014 Budget of the U.S. Government, United States Office of Management and Budget*, www.whitehouse.ogv/omb/budget/Historicals. Also see Robert J. Lieber, *Power and Willpower in the American Future*, tables 5.1 and 5.2, pp. 123–125.

[50] Stephen Sestanovich provides details and context and argues that NATO expansion into Eastern Europe and the Baltic region was not the primary cause in prompting Putin's virulent aggressive and anti-Western policies. See, "Could It Have Been Otherwise," *The American Interest*, Vol. X, No. 5 (May/June 2015), pp. 7–15. In contrast, Michael Mandelbaum argues that in the absence of NATO enlargement, Russia would not have adopted such confrontational policies, despite its shift to authoritarianism in domestic politics. See *Mission Failure: America and the World, 1993–2014* (New York: Oxford University Press, 2016), chapters 1 and 6.

[51] Dunford testimony to US Senate Armed Services Committee, quoted in "General Dunford's Common Sense," *FPI Bulletin*, Foreign Policy Initiative, July 13, 2015, www.foreignpolicyi.org/files/2015-07-13-Bulletin-General Dunford's Common Sense.pdf.

A further problem can be found in the disconnect between cuts in defense capability and the strategic doctrine that the armed forces are meant to serve. The annual National Security Strategy (NSS) and the accompanying National Military Strategy exemplify these problems of strategy and concept. The NSS is an annual presidential statement required since the passage in 1986 of the Goldwater–Nichols Act. In it, the president is required to submit to Congress a "comprehensive description and discussion" of America's grand strategy, setting out US interests, goals, and capabilities. In practice, these reports have often consisted of boilerplate restatements of official policy, though there have been exceptions, as in the case of NSC-68, Paul Nitze's classified report to President Harry Truman in 1950, describing a global threat from the Soviet Union that required a major American military buildup to implement the doctrine of containment. President Clinton's first NSS in 1993, although far less dramatic, described his administration's doctrine of "engagement and enlargement." And a year after 9/11, President George W. Bush's September 2002 National Security Strategy made the case for American primacy, preemption, and what came to be known as the Bush Doctrine.[52]

In this light, the Obama strategy documents offered general statements that tended not to address questions of capabilities, priorities, or resources. The 2015 National Security Strategy emphasized "strategic patience" and cooperation to support a rule-based world order. However, it did so with very broad language and few specifics, as when it called for leveraging national influence and economic growth and staying true to our values at home while advancing universal principles abroad. It proclaimed that, "First and foremost we will lead with purpose." And in citing the "top strategic risks," it listed broad categories but without indicating priorities among them. These included:

- Catastrophic attack on the US homeland or critical infrastructure;
- Threats or attacks against US citizens abroad and our allies;
- Global economic crisis or widespread economic slowdown;
- Proliferation and/or use of weapons of mass destruction;
- Severe global infectious disease outbreaks;
- Climate change;
- Major energy market disruptions; and
- Significant security consequences associated with weak or failing states (including mass atrocities, regional spillover, and transnational organized crime).[53]

Not only were these "top" risks not prioritized, but the NSS set out an expansive list of broad generalities without any indication of costs, programs, or plans. These included, "Put Our Economy to Work," "Advance Our Energy

---

[52] I assess the Bush Doctrine in Robert J. Lieber, *The American Era: Power and Strategy for the 21st Century* (New York: Cambridge University Press, 2007).

[53] *National Security Strategy*, February 2015, The White House (Washington, DC), p. 8.

Security," "Lead in Science, Technology," "Shape the Global Economic Order," "End Extreme Poverty," "Live Our Values," "Advance Equality," "Support Emerging Democracies," "Empower Civil Society and Young Leaders," "Seek Stability and Peace in the Middle East and North Africa," and others.[54]

The NSS thus did not provide a workable sense of strategic direction, and related subsidiary documents also had limited value. The Quadrennial Defense Review, known as the QDR, mainly offered a wish list and a number of broad strategic goals without a particular focus.[55] In turn, the National Military Strategy (NMS) is supposed to describe how an administration, and specifically the military, proposes to deal with the global challenges it identifies. The document, released in July 2015 by General Martin Dempsey, the then outgoing Chairman of the Joint Chiefs of Staff, offered little in specific response to the threats it identified, even while it was unusually candid in describing increasing dangers for the United States. Dempsey introduced the document by describing the global security environment as, "the most unpredictable that I have seen in 40 years," adding that, "global disorder has significantly increased while some of our comparative military advantage has begun to erode."[56] Russia, Iran, North Korea, and China were described as revisionist powers in explicit language as "attempting to revise key aspects of the international order and are acting in a manner that threatens our national security interest."[57] The document was surpassingly candid about the risk of war. In its words, "Today, the probability of US involvement in interstate war with a major power is assessed to be low but growing."[58]

The National Military Strategy also exhibited a glaring rhetorical omission, almost certainly reflecting the writ of the White House in its linguistic diffidence. In what was otherwise a commendably frank assessment of the geopolitical environment, the NMS never once referred to radical Islamism or radical Islamist terrorism. The closest it comes was in a single reference to "al Qaeda and the self-proclaimed Islamic State of Iraq and the Levant (ISIL)." Instead, it coined an Orwellian euphemism, "violent extremist organizations" (VEOs), an acronym which it then used seventeen times in the document's eighteen pages of text.[59]

---

[54] *Ibid.*, pp. 15–27.

[55] See, for example, the critical assessment of the QDR by Anthony H. Cordesman, "Strategy, Grand Strategy, and the Emperor's New Clothes," Center for Strategic and International Studies, Washington, DC, March 17, 2015, http://csis.org/publication/strategy-grand-strategy-and-emperors-new-clothes.

[56] *The National Military Strategy of the United States of America 2015: The United States Military's Contribution To National Security*, June 2015, p. i, www.jcs.mil/Portals/36/Documents/Publications/2015_National_Military_Strategy.pdf.

[57] *Ibid.*, p. 2.

[58] *Ibid.*, p. 4. And see Peter D. Feaver's analysis of the document, "How to Read the New National Military Strategy," *Foreignpolicy.com*, July 6, 2015, http://foreignpolicy.com/2015/07/06/how-to-read-the-new-national-military-strategy/.

[59] *The National Military Strategy of the United States of America 2015*, pp. 3, ff.

CONSEQUENCES FORESEEN AND UNFORESEEN

The combined effects of these defense cuts on American military readiness and force modernization, together with broader policies aimed at reducing America's foreign commitments and President Obama's own expressed preference for the United States to play a less assertive global role, had tangible effects on America's credibility. In ways large and small, both major powers such as China and Russia, and lesser ones such as Iran and North Korea, were becoming more assertive and less inclined to be deterred from actions the United States was known to oppose. *The Economist* put this shift succinctly:

Since the end of the cold war one simple geopolitical rule has endured: do not take on America. The country's armed forces have been so well resourced and so technologically superior that it would be utterly foolish for any state to mount a direct challenge to the superpower or its allies. This rule still holds – but it is no longer quite as compelling as it once was. Although America still possesses by far the most capable armed forces in the world, the technological advantage that guarantees it can defeat any conceivable adversary is ending rapidly.[60]

The result is not only a problem for the United States, but has serious world order consequences. Western-created institutions, norms, and rules have been backed by assumptions about American power. These beliefs were sufficiently pervasive that the realities were rarely tested. Now with American power and credibility no longer incontestable, the stability and durability of this rule-based international order should no longer be taken for granted.

There is ample evidence about the adverse consequences of retrenchment and inaction. Engagement, diplomacy, negotiation, international cooperation, and sanctions all have their uses as tools of foreign policy, but the most urgent and dangerous crises often require more assertive policies. In Ukraine, Syria, Iraq, Libya, and elsewhere, the unwillingness to take stronger measures has been harmful and the accompanying signals of inaction and lack of resolve have reverberated well beyond these areas. Geopolitical disarray and disorder have significantly worsened, a reality testified to by the leaders of America's intelligence agencies, military services, defense department, and – at times – the State Department.

Retrenchment and inaction have been harmful to regional order and to the security and national interests of the United States. In practice they have led not to more involvement and cooperation by others, but to less. And at the same time, confidence in the United States and deference to its ideals, preferences, and interests have waned. This is not always a matter of the use of force, and mostly not of dispatching American combat troops, but of how and in what circumstances power is used. In Ukraine the need was for defensive weapons, credible support for allies, and stronger more explicit condemnation of Russian aggression. In Syria, the issue was early training and support for

60 "Who's Afraid of America?" *The Economist*, June 13, 2015.

moderate rebels, and later making good on Obama's words that "the worst chemical attack of the 21st century ... must be confronted." In Iraq, the matter was one of avoiding a withdrawal that did not sacrifice what had been achieved at the cost of so much blood and treasure. And for the people of Libya the need was to work with others in supporting efforts to build a stable future after the fall of a capricious tyrant.

6

Can America still lead – and should it?

No major issue of world peace and stability can be resolved without US leadership.
– Lee Kwan Yew[1]

The foreign policy role of the United States matters greatly, not just for the prosperity and security of the country itself, but for the safety and security of America's allies and the future of global order. We tend to take for granted the institutions and rules of the road through which relations among nations take place, but these have been a product of the post–World War II international order largely created by American leadership in cooperation with wartime allies. It is thus fitting that a high ranking participant in these endeavors, Dean Acheson, who served as Under Secretary and then Secretary of State from 1949 to 1953, could entitle his memoir of that era, *Present at the Creation.*[2] Not only are the institutions such as the United Nations, International Monetary Fund, World Bank, NATO, European Union, World Trade Organization, International Court of Justice, World Health Organization, a direct or indirect product of that era, but so too are key elements of international law and the conduct of state to state relations involving sovereignty, territorial integrity, nonintervention, trade, travel, investment, and the principles (if not the observance) of human rights.

CRISES AND RESILIENCE

The viability as well as the desirability of America's leading international role came into question as early as the 1970s. As noted in Chapter 4, President

---

[1] Former Singapore Prime Minister Lee Kwan Yew, quoted in Peggy Noonan, "A Statesman's Friendly Advice," *Wall Street Journal*, June 7, 2013.
[2] Dean Acheson, *Present at the Creation: My Years in the State Department* (New York: Norton, 1969).

Richard Nixon and his National Security Advisor (and later Secretary of State) Henry Kissinger saw a need to adapt to a growing diffusion of power in the international system. The changes they identified included the postwar recovery of the Soviet Union with its formidable conventional and nuclear military power, the rejuvenation of the Europeans and Japan from the devastation of World War II and their appearance as major economic competitors to the United States, and the emergence of major regional powers in Asia, Africa, and Latin America. At the same time Nixon and Kissinger sought a means to disengage credibly from the Vietnam War and to mitigate the conflict with the Soviet Union through the policy of detente.

The United States had led the Western world since 1945, underwriting economic recovery, the NATO alliance, and geopolitical containment of the Soviet Union that allowed the industrial democracies to thrive as never before. But with the passage of time, the power position the United States had enjoyed in the immediate years after World War II was no longer so predominant. America still retained enormous resources of military, economic, and diplomatic power, but its geopolitical standing and its economic and energy predominance faced challenges in those years. For the first time since the end of World War II, the United States ran a balance of trade deficit, and in August 1971 Nixon ended the convertibility of the dollar into gold at the fixed exchange rate of $35 per ounce and imposed a temporary surcharge on imported goods. These and other changes during the early 1970s brought an end to the Bretton Woods system of fixed exchange rates that had been created in cooperation with allied countries in 1944.

Still more dramatically, the Yom Kippur War of October 1973, in which Egypt and Syria launched a surprise attack against Israel, led to an oil embargo against the United States by major Arab oil producing countries. The embargo and oil production cuts by these producers created a global shortfall of some 7 percent of world demand.[3] By the time the embargo and production cuts ended, the Organization of Petroleum Exporting Countries (OPEC) had taken advantage of the crisis to quadruple the price of oil, from $2.70 per barrel on the eve of the October War to $10.40 in March 1974.[4] The oil shock delivered a serious economic blow to the United States and the major oil importing countries. As a group, the members of the Organization for Economic Cooperation

---

[3] It should be noted that the embargo and production cuts were undertaken by the Organization of *Arab* Oil Exporting Countries (OAPEC), not OPEC itself, a distinction that still eludes some authors and commentators. For an account of the 1973–4 oil crisis and its aftermath, see Robert J. Lieber, *The Oil Decade: Conflict and Cooperation in the West* (New York: Praeger, 1983), pp. 13–43.

[4] Figures for the official selling price of Saudi Arabian light marker crude oil, at that time the *de facto* benchmark price for OPEC oil. Source: Exon Corporation, *Middle East Oil* (New York: Exon Background Series, September 1980), p. 26. Also see US Department of Energy, Energy Information Administration, *Weekly Petroleum Status Review*, June 5, 1981, DOE/EIA-0208 (81/23), p. 20.

and Development (OECD) suffered a major recession and from 1973 to 1974 saw their net oil import bill rise from $35 billion to over $100 billion.[5] More importantly, the oil shock touched off worries that a profound transformation in the world economy might be taking place, ending a generation of extraordinary growth in North America, Europe, and Japan, and presaging a shift in world economic power from North to South.

In reality, writing the epitaph for the advanced industrial democracies proved entirely premature. Moreover, the Nixon administration retained important economic, diplomatic, and military measures of influence, and in a deft move achieved a dramatic opening to the Peoples' Republic of China, with which the United States had been at loggerheads since the Communists' 1949 victory over the Nationalists in the Chinese civil war. In playing the China card, Nixon and Kissinger were able to exert significant leverage against Moscow.

Nonetheless, the international standing of the United States seemed to worsen during the remainder of the 1970s. In August 1974, President Richard Nixon resigned in disgrace as a result of the Watergate scandal and was succeeded by Gerald Ford. Nixon had ended the American ground combat role in Vietnam in 1972, but in June 1973 Democratic majorities in the House and Senate halted the use of American airpower and then in December 1974 cut off all military assistance to the South Vietnamese forces.[6] In April 1975, the last Americans withdrew from South Vietnam as North Vietnamese troops closed in on Saigon. Though US troops had never been defeated militarily, they had failed to prevent the Communist takeover of South Vietnam despite more than a decade of war, hundreds of billions of dollars in aid to South Vietnam, and the loss of 58,000 American lives. The outcome was widely seen as a major defeat for the United States. The loss of Vietnam was quickly followed by the fall of Cambodia and Laos. In addition, there were advances in the developing world by Soviet-supported revolutionary movements, in Angola and Mozambique, where Cuban combat troops intervened, as well as in Ethiopia, Nicaragua, El Salvador, Yemen, and elsewhere.

Other urgent catalysts for change arose too. One of the most important of these took place in early November 1979, when a mob of young Islamist radicals seized the US embassy in Tehran and took its occupants hostage.

---

[5] Data from *OECD World Economic Outlook*, pp. 121–123.

[6] In June 1973, Congress passed the Case-Church amendment by a veto-proof margin. This terminated US military involvement in Vietnam, most importantly the use of American air power. In December 2014, following the November election in which Democrats gained 49 seats; Congress eliminated all military aid to Vietnam, leaving in place only modest economic assistance. In March 1975, North Vietnamese forces invaded South Vietnam with eighteen army divisions equipped with Soviet tanks. Without US aid, South Vietnamese forces ran out of ammunition and petroleum. Saigon fell to the North Vietnamese on April 30, 1975. See, for example, Lewis Sorley, *A Better War: The Unexamined Victories and Final Tragedy of America's Last Years in Vietnam* (New York: Harcourt Brace, 1999); Melvin Laird, "Iraq: Learning the Lessons of Vietnam," *Foreign Affairs*, November/December 2005.

A number of the detainees, especially women, were released, but fifty-two of them remained. Initially, the Carter administration imposed economic sanctions and diplomatic pressure on Iran but otherwise appeared uncertain how to respond. Finally, in April 1980 it launched a high-risk rescue attempt, Operation Eagle Claw. The attempt ended in disaster at Desert One, a site in Iran's Great Salt Desert some fifty miles from Tehran. Two American aircraft collided in the midst of a sandstorm, killing eight airmen and causing the mission to be aborted. The hostages were only released after 444 days in captivity, moments after President Carter left office.

Still another dramatic event came with the Soviet invasion of Afghanistan on December 27, 1979. During its first three years in office, the Carter administration had sought to de-emphasize the Cold War, but Soviet leaders instead worked to exploit what they perceived as an emerging shift in the worldwide correlation of forces. In Marxist-Leninist language, Soviet ideologues believed that the underlying balance of power, in military, geopolitical, and material terms, had turned in their favor and that, in view of American weaknesses (Watergate, Vietnam, reductions in US military forces, decision to relinquish control of the Panama Canal, the Iran hostage crisis), now was the time to exploit that momentum.[7] Meanwhile, Moscow adhered to the Brezhnev Doctrine, made explicit in 1968 in the aftermath of its invasion of Czechoslovakia, proclaiming the right of the Soviet Union and its allies to intervene in the affairs of Soviet bloc countries, "when forces that are hostile to socialism try to turn the development of some socialist country towards capitalism." Insightful – and witty – observers of the Soviets, labeled the doctrine as meaning, "What's mine is mine, what's yours is negotiable."

President Carter reacted by taking steps to arm the Afghan resistance to the Soviets and to increase the defense budget which had been cut significantly in the aftermath of Vietnam. Then in January 1980, he announced what came to be called the Carter Doctrine, asserting that any attempt by an outside power to gain control of the Persian Gulf region would be regarded as an assault on America's vital interests and "would be repelled by any means necessary including military force."[8]

This trend of strategic reassertion was intensified under President Ronald Reagan, who took office in January 1981. Whereas three previous presidents, Richard Nixon, Gerald Ford, and Jimmy Carter, had sought to adapt foreign policy to foreign constraints and an increasing diffusion of power, Reagan sought to overcome these constraints through major foreign and domestic policy changes. He accelerated the increases in defense spending and the

---

[7] Raymond L. Garthoff, "The Concept of the Balance of Power in Soviet Policy Making," *World Politics*, October 1951, pp. 87–93; and Mackubin T. Owens, "The 'Correlation of Forces,' Then and Now," (Ashland, OH: Ashbrook Ashland University, Publications, February 2004), http://ashbrook.org/publications/oped-owens-04-cof/

[8] President Jimmy Carter, State of the Union Address, January 23, 1980, http://millercenter.org/president/carter/speeches/speech-3404.

rebuilding of American conventional and nuclear forces. In addition, he reasserted American power in the developing world by expanding military and economic assistance to forces battling against pro-Soviet regimes as well as to local governments threatened by pro-Soviet movements. Together, these policies became known as the Reagan Doctrine. At home, Reagan promoted changes in domestic economic policy including painful steps to reverse high inflation, coupled with tax cuts and efforts to reduce governmental regulation.

In addition to these foreign policy measures, Reagan called for a Strategic Defense Initiative (soon dubbed by its critics as "Star Wars"). In a March 1983 address, he proposed development of an antimissile system that might one day protect the United States from nuclear attack. At the time, much of the advanced technology was unavailable, let alone deployable. Nonetheless, the proposal, along with the Reagan Doctrine and the heavy burdens of an accelerating arms race, played a significant role in persuading the new Soviet leader, Mikhail Gorbachev, to welcome negotiations with Washington that would ultimately bring an end to the Cold War. The reasons for the transformation in Soviet policy remain a subject of debate among strategists and historians, and no one cause is likely to have been decisive in itself. Nonetheless, Gorbachev's own words to the Soviet Politburo in 1986 capture his sense of Soviet vulnerability and his fears about the inability to sustain an intensified competition with the United States:

Our goal is to prevent the next round of the arms race. If we do not accomplish it, the threat to us will only grow. We will be pulled into another round of the arms race that is beyond our capabilities, and we will lose it, because we are already at the limit of our capabilities. Moreover, we can expect that Japan and the FRG [West Germany] could very soon join the American potential ... If the new round begins, the pressure on our economy will be unbelievable.[9]

The Gorbachev statement and especially the end of the Cold War itself should serve as reminders about the tendency to underestimate the underlying strengths of the United States, even at times when it is subject to formidable challenges abroad or deep difficulties at home.

WEIGHING THE US POST-COLD WAR AND POST-9/11 ROLES

With the end of the Cold War a quarter-century ago, and especially after the start of the twenty-first century, many observers, not only abroad but within the United States itself, argued that the United States should or would play a lesser role in a much more globalized and multipolar world. But while international

---

[9] Politburo session of October 4, 1986, in National Security Archive Briefing Book, *Understanding the End of the Cold War: The Reagan/Gorbachev Years* (Providence, RI: Brown University, 1998), quoted in Stephen G. Brooks and William C. Wohlforth, "Power, Globalization, and the End of the Cold War: Reevaluating a Landmark Case for Ideas," *International Security*, Vol. 25, No. 3 (Winter 2000/01), pp. 5–53 at p. 29.

law, the UN, the EU, the Association of Southeast Asian Nations (ASEAN), the BRICS, the WTO, and a multiplicity of international institutions and regimes all matter in the conduct of international relations, the record of recent decades provides ample evidence of their limitations. This is not just a matter of shared responsibility, but at certain times and in specific places it is one of war and peace or life and death.

Though the active engagement of the United States is not a sufficient condition for world order, it is often a necessary one. The cases in which this has been evident are numerous and it is sobering to be reminded of some of the most conspicuous examples of what happens when America is absent. In Syria, the regime of Bashar al-Assad repeatedly used poison gas against its own population during the civil war which began in 2011. Despite the moral opprobrium, Assad acted with impunity. This is all the more striking given the existence of the Chemical Weapons Convention (CWC, officially, the Convention on the Prohibition of the Development, Production, Stockpiling and Use of Chemical Weapons). This international treaty, adopted in 1992, entered into force in 1997 and has been signed by 189 countries including Russia and the United States. Moreover, to implement its provisions, the Organization for the Prohibition of Chemical Weapons (OPCW) was created in cooperation with the UN to monitor, implement, verify, and "to provide protection and assistance against chemical weapons."[10]

As with almost all international agreements, the CWC is not self-enforcing. The UN Security Council lacks the unity among its permanent members to do so and the OPCW does not have the authority or capacity to act. Russia, as an ally and weapons supplier of Syria, was not inclined to take measures against Assad, nor was Syria's chief regional supporter, Iran. Among the permanent members of the Security Council, China is leery of intervention in the internal affairs of others, and Britain and France might have been willing to take action, but only if led by the United States. However, President Obama's hesitant initial call to action was followed by the British Parliament's rejection of intervention, whereupon Washington backed away from using force to punish the Syrian regime and thus from any real enforcement of the red line.

At that point, with the Obama administration's use of force in abeyance and the President's threat in question, the Russians proposed an agreement for Syria to destroy its chemical weapons and production facilities and to join the Chemical Weapons Convention. As a powerful backer of the Syrian regime, Moscow had considerable leverage with Assad. The Obama administration found the measure a welcome way out of its policy dilemma, and the deal was agreed to in September 2013. These steps were to have been completed by June 2014, and Syria did hand over large quantities of the munitions. Nonetheless, within months of the deadline, international inspectors reported that Assad's forces had

[10] For a detailed description, see "Chemical Weapons," United Nations Office for Disarmament Affairs, www.un.org/disarmament/WMD/Chemical/.

again resorted to using poison gas, in the form of barrel bombs filled with chlorine. They did so, however, at a time of other crises for US policymakers, involving Russia in Ukraine, ISIS in Syria and Iraq, China in the East and South China Seas and – most importantly for the Obama administration – nuclear negotiations with Iran. As a result, the Obama administration largely sidestepped the Syria chemical weapons issue.

In the case of Ukraine and Crimea, discussed in Chapter 2, the Budapest Memorandum of 1994 had offered Ukraine guarantees of its territorial integrity and security, yet despite the signatures of the five permanent members of the Security Council, the agreement proved to be a dead letter when, two decades later, Ukraine appealed for help against Russia's violations of its borders and sovereignty. Nor did older and more venerable agreements and treaties such as the Helsinki Final Act of 1975 or the UN Charter offer any effective relief.

The case of Libya is consistent with this pattern. The United States did play a key role in the early phase of the 2011 conflict, despite "leading from behind," but it disengaged after the fall of Gaddafi and did not take meaningful steps to assist in the establishment of an effective new government or to rally allies or regional actors to do so. Although the UN Security Council had provided international legitimacy for the military effort in Libya, with Resolution 1973 passed on March 17, 2011 and authorizing "all necessary measures" to protect civilians and establish a no-fly zone against the Gaddafi regime, the UN itself did not provide an effective institutional framework for sustaining order in post-Gaddafi Libya. Moreover, none of the major international or regional powers were willing to do so. The result was a deteriorating situation with increasing hostilities among local authorities and regional militias, and the intrusion of jihadist groups into the conflict. Amid the chaos, Libya became a launching spot for human traffickers, sending boatloads of desperate refugees across the Mediterranean toward Europe and with great loss of life. Increasingly, Libya became a recruiting and training round for al-Qaeda and the Islamic State (ISIS).

Two earlier cases from the 1990s and the Clinton administration provide comparable evidence both of the often lethal inadequacy of international agreements and institutions and of the consequences when the United States chooses not to engage. One of these was the notorious Srebrenica massacre during the civil war in Bosnia.[11] In 1993, the UN Security Council had declared the Bosnian Muslim town of Srebrenica a "safe area." Yet in July 1995, despite the town being garrisoned by a battalion of Dutch troops wearing UN blue helmets, driving white-painted vehicles, and displaying the UN flag, Serb militias under the command of Bosnian Serb General Radko Mladic overran the town. Over the course of several days they rounded up and executed at least

---

[11] The case of Srebrenica is dealt with in detail in Samantha Power, *"A Problem from Hell": America and the Age of Genocide* (New York: Basic Books, 2002), pp. 401–435. I elaborate on this in Robert J. Lieber, *Power and Willpower in the American Future*, chapter four.

7,000 Bosnian Muslim men and boys – the worst atrocity in Europe since the end of World War II. Fifteen years later, in 2010, four Bosnian Serb military officials were convicted at the International Criminal Tribunal for the former Yugoslavia (ICTY), located in The Hague. In 2015 General Mladic himself finally faced charges of war crimes and genocide in the same tribunal.

Another and far more deadly case was the Rwanda genocide of April–July 1994, in which as many as 700,000 Tutsis and 100,000 moderate Hutus were slaughtered by Hutu militias. Here too, the United States refused to support a meaningful international response. As the killing began, Washington actually prodded the Security Council into cutting the size of its UN peacekeeping contingent, UNAMIR, from 2,500 men to 500. Six months earlier, the Clinton administration had been stunned by the Blackhawk Down incident in Mogadishu, Somalia, where eighteen US Army Rangers had been killed. They had been present under a UN mandate, and the administration had faced withering criticism for its handling of the intervention. Not only did the Clinton administration not intervene to stop the Rwanda killing, but as Samantha Power observes, "it blocked the deployment of UN peacekeepers, and it refrained from undertaking softer forms of intervention."[12] Clinton's foreign policymakers also sought to discourage use of the word "genocide" for fear that it might motivate the American public to support intervention. In sum, in this case as in others, the alternative to serious involvement by the United States in urgent and deadly crises was not that the UN, some other multilateral institution, or another powerful state would take the lead in maintaining order, but that the alternative was more likely to be inaction and often tragedy.

A great deal thus depends on whether the United States still can provide international leadership. But contrary to arguments that the relevant policy choice is one of diplomacy *or* military force, the two dimensions are often related and reinforcing. In the case of diplomacy, exhortations not backed up with the substance of power are empty and can have unintended consequences in undermining America's credibility with adversaries as well as with allies. The Syria "red line" fiasco is a case in point, as was Obama's statement that described Putin's actions in Ukraine as unacceptable in the twenty-first-century world. Both statements were devoid of consequences. In essence, as strategic thinkers over the ages have observed, power without diplomacy is blind, but diplomacy without power is impotent.[13] Power is not just or even mainly military power projection and "boots on the ground," but the credible willingness of a country to underwrite its diplomacy with the resources it

---

[12] Power, *A Problem from Hell*, p. 373.

[13] In the words of Hans Morgenthau, "Remember that diplomacy without power is feeble, and power without diplomacy is destructive and blind." *In Defense of the National Interest: A Critical Examination of American Foreign Policy* (New York: Knopf, 1951), pp. 241–242. Prussia's Frederick the Great (1712–86) is credited with saying, "Diplomacy without military power is like music without instruments."

commands: economic, technological, political, moral, and if necessary, military. For America, this leads to the question of whether, in the aftermath of financial crises and grinding and inconclusive wars in Afghanistan and Iraq during the past decade, the country still possesses the will as well as the capacity to play a leading international role.

AMERICA AND THE IDEA OF DECLINE

Despite America's formidable material strengths, the specter of decline has reappeared throughout much of the country's history.[14] During the nineteenth century there were five major economic and financial crises as well as the Civil War, which itself raised questions about whether the United States would survive as a unified country. In the twentieth century, the challenges included two massive world wars and the great depression of the 1930s which, in the words of President Franklin Roosevelt, left "one-third of a nation ill-housed, ill-clad, ill-nourished," and caused some to wonder whether American democracy itself could survive.[15] And there have been regional wars, costly in blood and treasure, in Korea, Vietnam, Afghanistan, and Iraq, as well the September 11, 2001 terrorist attack on New York and Washington.

In the seven decades since World War II, America has experienced several periods in which many believed the country was entering an era of national decline. In at least three of these cases, this was not just a matter of economic trouble, but of a rising challenger thought to be outpacing America. The earliest of these episodes took place after the Soviets successfully launched the first man-made space object, the Soyuz satellite, in October 1957. Fear that the Russians might be pulling ahead in the space race suggested dangers in the arms competition too. Critics complained that America's math and science lagged in comparison with those of the Soviets, that its children were lazy, unfocused, and undisciplined, and that the country needed a new impetus. Yet the following years saw a massive expansion in higher education, a speed up in conventional and nuclear weapons programs, and a commitment made by President John Kennedy to put a man on the moon by the end of the 1960s – an achievement successfully realized in July 1969.

There were other reversals too. In the late 1970s, in the aftermath of Vietnam and losses in the developing world, there were again fears that the Soviets were pulling ahead. A decade later the Soviet challenge was replaced by concern over a rising Japan, whose competitiveness, along with its quality cars and electronics and its quest to buy prime US properties seemed for a time unstoppable.

---

[14] This discussion of American decline elaborates upon arguments I made in *Power and Willpower in the American Future: Why The United States is Not Destined to Decline* (New York: Cambridge, 2012).

[15] Franklin D. Roosevelt, Second Inaugural Address, January 20, 1937.

It was during the period of the Japanese challenge that Paul Kennedy published his best-seller, *The Rise and Fall of the Great Powers*.[16] In it, the author warned against the dangers of imperial overstretch, in which a great empire's foreign commitments could come to overburden its economy and society, thus leading to its decline. Playing to popular anxiety, the novelist Michael Crichton published *Rising Sun*, with its depiction of rising Japanese economic power and nefarious corporate takeovers.[17]

Ironically, by the early 1990s, Japan had fallen into a two-decade period of economic difficulty, the Cold War ended, the Soviet Union collapsed, and an entirely new set of concerns began to be heard. Now, America was depicted as becoming dangerously dominant. More recently, in the immediate aftermath of the 2008–09 financial crisis and at a time when the United States had not yet begun its withdrawal from wars in Afghanistan and Iraq, China became the country now threatening to surpass America if, indeed, it had not already done so. This phenomenon too has showed signs of easing as China's economic growth has slowed from its double digit pace and that of the United States has improved, but references to the idea of China's rise and America's decline remain commonplace. Thus an even cursory glance at Google and the words, "Decline of America" produces nearly 200 million hits. For its part, even the American public remains skeptical about national performance, with more than 60 percent consistently describing the country as on the "wrong track."[18]

Exaggerated treatments and pessimistic interpretations of America's future can be easy to caricature, but sober and well-regarded experts have not been immune from alarmism. Consider, for example, the words of one of the country's most respected strategic thinkers, Henry Kissinger:

[T]he United States cannot afford another decline like that which has characterized the past decade and a half ... [O]nly self-delusion can keep us from admitting our decline to ourselves.

The observation seems ominous, yet Kissinger wrote those words not in recent years, but more than a half-century ago, in his 1961 book, *The Necessity for Choice*.[19]

The explanation for these repeated cycles of declinist sentiment seem to lie in a propensity toward short-term thinking, overreaction to adversity and, most importantly, insufficient appreciation for the resilience and adaptability of the United States in coping with crises. To be sure, the United States does face serious problems. Though the most acute of the major economic and

---

[16] Paul Kennedy, *Economic Change and Military Conflict from 1500 to 2000* (New York: Random, 1987).

[17] Michael Crichton, *Rising Sun* (New York: Knopf, 1992).

[18] www.realclearpolitics.com/, accessed January 26, 2016.

[19] Henry A. Kissinger, *The Necessity for Choice: Prospects of American Foreign Policy* (New York: Harper, 1961), pp. 1–2.

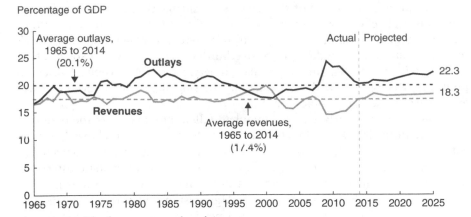

FIGURE 6.1 Total revenues and outlays
Source: Congressional Budget Office (CBO), The Budget and Economic Outlook: 2015
to 2025, Report, January 26, 2015, www.cbo.gov/publication/49892.

financial difficulties from the 2008–9 crisis have been largely alleviated, a list
of important domestic and foreign concerns remains.

On the home front, the most long term of these worries involves the domestic budget deficit. As recently as 2010, the gap between total federal revenues
and outlays had widened to an unsustainable 10 percent of GDP. However,
over the following five years, the deficit dropped to 2.5 percent of GDP, a figure
actually lower than the average of 3.0 percent for the pre-financial crisis period
from 1971 to 2007 (see Figure 6.1).

There is a risk of complacency, however, in examining these numbers. An
immediate problem is that the bipartisan budget agreement known as the
"sequester" resulted in damaging cuts of $500 billion each from defense and
from nondiscretionary spending. These were enacted in the Budget Control
Act of 2011, which took effect in 2013. The legislation sought to reduce federal spending by more than $1 trillion over an eight-year period. As a result of
these and other defense budget cuts, the size of the Army has been reduced by
100,000 soldiers, the Navy faces serious backlogs in maintenance and readiness, fewer than half the Air Force's combat squadrons are combat ready, and
half of nondeployed Marine Corps units lack personnel, equipment, or training. In the four-year period 2011–14, real defense spending fell 21 percent and,
in the absence of policy change, scheduled reductions in spending and troop
levels and weapons procurement over several years will reduce the military's
share of GDP to the lowest level since before America's entry into World War II.

These reductions in defense spending, weapons programs, and troop levels
need to be set against long-standing US foreign policy commitments. Under
Article 5 of the North Atlantic Treaty, the United States is committed to come to

the aid of the twenty-seven other countries of NATO if they are attacked. Given the depredations of Putin's Russia against Georgia and Ukraine (non-NATO members), but also his threats to the NATO Baltic countries (Latvia, Lithuania, and Estonia), as well as menacing overflights and naval incursions directed at Poland and a number of northern European NATO countries, the commitment is important for regional stability. In addition, America has formal obligations to the defense of South Korea, where Secretary of State John Kerry has proclaimed America's "ironclad commitment" to its security and where the United States still stations nearly 30,000 troops more than six decades after the end of the Korean War.[20] "Ironclad commitment" is also a term that was used by President Obama to reassure the Persian Gulf sheikhdoms and Saudi Arabia, themselves anxious about Iran and its proxies, that the United States would "use all elements of its power … to deter and confront external aggression" against them.[21]

Those are by no means the only commitments that ultimately rest on the deterrence and defense provided by the United States. In addition, President Obama repeatedly reassured Israel, which remains deeply concerned about threats from Iran and the risk of it eventually acquiring nuclear weapons. In Obama's words, "The people of Israel must always know America has its back."[22] President Obama also committed the United States to the support of Saudi Arabian forces in the Yemen conflict and to the eventual defeat of ISIS in Iraq and Syria. On a much larger scale, though largely undefined in specific terms, the "pivot to Asia" implies not only backing for existing East Asian allies (Japan, South Korea, Australia, the Philippines), but also a potentially open-ended commitment regarding free passage through areas of the East and South China Seas claimed by China.

On the domestic side, the cuts do not affect entitlement programs, but they have had an impact on nondefense discretionary spending for scientific research and development. For example, as a result of previous budget decisions and adjusted for inflation, the National Institutes of Health are estimated to have lost nearly 25 percent of their purchasing power in the past decade.[23] Infrastructure including roads, ports, bridges, and airports, has been underfunded, and the resulting bottlenecks and inefficiencies are harmful to productivity.

Despite a welcome reduction in the annual federal budget deficit, the figure is projected to worsen significantly after the end of the decade. At that point,

---

[20] "Ironclad commitment" quoted in Carol Morello, "Kerry to Reassure Seoul on Security Backing from U.S.," *Washington Post*, May 18, 2015.

[21] Quoted in Fred Hiatt, "A Military Budget for the Real World," *Washington Post*, May 18, 2015.

[22] President Obama's address to some 1,200 people, including members of Congress, at a Washington synagogue, Congregation Adas Israel, May 22, 2015, quoted in Darlene Superville, "Obama: Disagreement between US, Israel does not signal lack of US support for long-time ally," Associated Press and US News, May 22, 2015, www.usnews.com/news/politics/articles/2015/05/22/obama-to-address-anti-semitism-at-jewish-congregation.

[23] The estimate is that of NIH head, Francis Collins, cited in Robert Samuelson, "The Twisted Priorities of a Graying Nation," *Washington Post*, February 8, 2015.

the growing costs of entitlement programs will put increasing pressure on the budget. Major reforms are needed to adjust benefits, age requirements, and contribution formulas in order to keep Social Security, Medicare, Medicaid, and veterans' benefits on a viable long-term trajectory. Failure to do so risks harming America's economy as well as constraining funds available for defense and foreign policy.

These are by no means the sole domestic problems facing the United States. For example, the International Monetary Fund has cut its estimate of America's potential growth rate to 2.0 percent per year, little more than half the level of two decades ago, a figure it describes as "weighed down by an aging population and weak innovation and productivity growth."[24] Corporate tax rates are higher than among any of America's major competitors and act as a disincentive to investment.

In addition, immigration remains a major and troubling concern. The dilemma here is how to cope with more than ten million illegal immigrants, many of whom have lived in the United States for considerable periods of time. The issue is bound up with questions of law, politics, and humanity, and it has proved difficult to resolve in a political atmosphere of intense partisanship. The problem not only concerns those who are already within the United States, but also the shaping of policy to facilitate immigration and citizenship for those with the skills to contribute successfully in a modern globalized economy and society.

Though often buried deep inside the business pages of major newspapers, problems of bureaucracy, regulation, and litigiousness pose problems, especially in the path of would-be startups and innovators. Recent data suggest that the United States has become somewhat less competitive and has seen its level of entrepreneurship erode as a consequence of often onerous, time-consuming, and redundant regulations. America has slipped from first to twelfth among developed countries in terms of business startup activity. In addition, for the first time in thirty-five years, the annual creation of new businesses is outnumbered by business failures.[25]

As but one among a multitude of examples, which would seemingly fit the satirical pages of *The Onion*, there was the widely reported case of a children's magician, one Marty Hahne ("Marty the Magician") of Ozark, Missouri, being obliged to prepare an elaborate disaster emergency plan for his rabbit. The US Department of Agriculture (USDA) had previously required that the rabbit be licensed; something the magician only learned when confronted by a badge-wielding USDA inspector. In the aftermath of Hurricane Katrina in 2005, USDA had proposed a regulation that all licensed exhibitors be required

---

[24] *World Economic Outlook*, April 2015, Washington, DC: International Monetary Fund, p. 47, www.imf.org/external/pubs/ft/weo/2015/01/index.htm.

[25] Jim Clifton, "American Entrepreneurship: Dead or Alive," *gallup.com.*, January 13, 2015, www.gallup.com/businessjournal/180431/american-entrepreneurship-dead-alive.aspx.

to write disaster plans. Though 95 percent of the nearly 1,000 people who sub-mitted comments opposed adoption of the rule, it nonetheless took effect on January 30, 2013. The law originally was intended to cover only large enter-prises including exhibitors such as zoos and circuses as well as pet dealers and laboratories. With the passage of time, however, the regulation had been expanded and its implementation widened so that USDA now had no fewer than fourteen pages of regulations intended just for rabbits.

The *Washington Post* ran a story about the magician, the rabbit, and the regulations, and in the glare of publicity, the Secretary of Agriculture suddenly intervened, announcing his department would "reexamine" the requirement.[26] Publicity and embarrassment in this case clearly had their effect, but examples of excessive and dysfunctional regulation are not in the least unusual – and most are not so amusing or so readily "reexamined." Reacting to the seemingly unrelenting proliferation of regulations, the historian Niall Ferguson goes so far as to warn that the institutions of representative government, the free mar-ket, the rule of law, and civil society are threatened, and that, "Western civili-zation has entered a period of decline due mainly to the entangling of private initiative by the ever-encroaching state."[27]

COMMITMENTS AND CAPABILITIES

Can the United States still play a leading role in world affairs? Some would say that doing so is undesirable, whether or not America possesses that capac-ity. In the earlier portions of this work, I have argued that realist arguments for disengagement and offshore balancing are profoundly unrealistic in their assumptions. These approaches devote insufficient weight to adversaries' motives, beliefs, ideologies, and history. That is, in accounting for how others will act, realists deprive them of agency in that they interpret their conduct as determined primarily in reaction to American policies or by the international distribution of power, more than by willful choices made by foreign leaders on their own volition. The realist assumption that local actors normally will tend to balance against threat or instability if the United States is absent is deeply flawed. It assumes an automaticity in human affairs that cannot be relied upon, and the accompanying notion that the United States can retreat comfortably and safely behind two oceans (realists refer to the "stopping power of water") embodies a stunning complacency.[28]

[26] David A. Fahrenthold, "Watch Him Pull a USDA-mandated Rabbit Disaster Plan out of His Hat," *Washington Post*, July 16. 2013.
[27] Quoted in George Melloan, "A Jeremiad to Heed," review of Niall Ferguson's *The Great Degeneration* (New York: Penguin, 2013), *Wall Street Journal*, June 20, 2013.
[28] The term was given currency by John J. Mearsheimer, *The Tragedy of Great Power Politics* (New York: Norton, 2001), p. 27. For a more recent reference to the "stopping power of water," see Stephen M. Walt, "Chill Out, America," *Foreign Policy*, May 28, 2015.

Those who instead emphasize international institutions as sources of order that can function without strong American engagement also face a conceptual problem. In this case, they overestimate the autonomous capacities of these bodies when not actively supported by powerful states. Egregious cases of the limits and outright failures of the UN, EU, OSCE, and others abound, not least Rwanda, Srebrenica, Syria, and Russia–Ukraine.

A key assumption on the part of those who are pessimistic about the ability of the United States to sustain its own leading world role is that America can no longer afford to do so. This idea follows from the logic of imperial overstretch, as for example in Paul Kennedy's writing cited earlier and the saga of British imperial decline. Other authors preceded Kennedy in describing an excess of overseas commitments as a central cause of imperial or great power decline. Drawing on cases such as those of Athens, Rome, the Netherlands, and Great Britain, Robert Gilpin identified the external (i.e., international) burdens as one of three main causes, along with rising domestic consumption and the diffusion of technology abroad.[29]

However, the evidence that international obligations currently create an excessive financial burden for the United States is limited. Military spending would seem to be the most relevant indicator, and a defense budget of $600 billion per year does represent an enormous sum of money. Nonetheless, as a share of GDP the burden is manageable when weighed against the experience of recent decades. Thus the figure for fiscal year 2015 was just 3.4 percent of GDP and has been projected to fall as low as 2.8 percent by 2018.[30] In contrast, the costs of defense averaged 10.4 percent of GDP during the 1950s, 8.7 percent in the 1960s, 5.9 and then 5.8 percent in the 1970s and 1980s, 4.0 percent in the 1990s, and 3.9 in the first decade of this century. The wars in Afghanistan and Iraq proved costly in terms of money and human lives, and expenditures for those conflicts peaked in 2011, with overall defense spending topping out at 5.1 percent of GDP. Nonetheless, the relative costs for defense have dropped quickly since that time. The international affairs budget (the State Department, foreign aid, international institutions) adds an additional $50 billion, and the substantial sums expended for the CIA as well as other intelligence agencies not included in the defense budget need to be taken into account as well. Nonetheless, in view of previous economic performance, competitiveness, and technological and scientific innovation, there is ample evidence that the United States is able to prosper despite the financial burdens of foreign commitments.

Not only is the relative weight of defense spending sustainable, but the case for decline is overstated and conceptually flawed when the experience of the

[29] Robert Gilpin, *War and Change in World Politics* (New York: Cambridge University Press, 1981).
[30] Data from table 6.1 Composition of Outlays: 1940–2018, "Historical Tables" and table 8.7 Outlays for Discretionary Programs: 1962–2018, "Historical Tables," *Fiscal Year 2014 Budget of the U.S. Government, United States Office of Management and Budget*, www.whitehouse.ogv/omb/budget/Historicals.

British Empire is cited as a precedent or a warning. The cases of Britain and the United States are not really comparable. More than a century ago in 1914, on the eve of World War I, Britain had already been overtaken by both the United States and Imperial Germany in industrial production, GDP, military spending, and troop strength.[31] In contrast, not only does the United States not bear the burden of maintaining colonies abroad, but it remains the world leader in almost all comparative measures of national power other than population, where it will continue to rank third after India and China.

AMERICA'S MATERIAL RESOURCES

In material terms, and without disregarding its sometimes daunting problems, America's strengths remain only modestly diminished compared with a generation ago. In terms of almost all the criteria by which power is measured, the country retains a unique international position. Beyond military power, these strengths include economic size, the depth and breadth of US financial markets, the role of the dollar (in which some 60 percent of world trade takes place), and a durable, stable rule of law that makes the United States a safe haven for investments. In addition, science and technology, innovation, competitiveness, energy, natural resources, agricultural productivity, demography, adaptability, openness, attractiveness to talented immigrants, and a host of other indicators reflect the overall health and strength of the economy and society. America leads the world in the number, depth, and caliber of its research universities and attracts enormous numbers of talented and ambitious foreign students. It tops the lists of awardees for the Nobel Prize in medicine, chemistry, physics, and economics. In commerce, American companies are world leaders in the digital age and in the technologies likely to be most in demand in the economies of the future.

Economic size is the most widely used indicator of national strength, and here misconceptions abound, especially concerning whether China is overtaking the United States or may already have done so. Chapter 4 provided an explanation of why gross domestic product (GDP) in terms of market exchange rates rather than purchasing power parity (PPP) remains the preferred indicator for international comparisons. If the share of world GDP is calculated in terms of purchasing power parity, IMF estimates for 2016 show China with a slightly larger percentage than that of the United States, 17.71 versus 15.78. However, based on the more relevant criterion of market exchange rates, the US share of world GDP is 24.50 still substantially ahead of China at 16.06. (See Tables 6.1 and 6.2)

---

[31] Aaron Friedberg made this point and provided the data in *The Weary Titan: Britain and the Experience of Relative Decline, 1895–1905* (Princeton, NJ: Princeton University Press, 1988), p. 26.

TABLE 6.1. *Share of world GDP at purchasing power parity**

Country	1992	1993	1994	1995	1996	1997	1998	1999	2000	2001	2002	2003	2004	2005	2006
United States	20.26	20.40	20.59	20.40	20.39	20.44	20.84	21.07	20.93	20.63	20.41	20.18	19.85	19.58	19.07
China	4.56	5.09	5.58	5.97	6.32	6.63	6.97	7.25	7.50	7.93	8.40	8.90	9.28	9.86	10.54
Japan	8.05	7.90	7.73	7.60	7.51	7.32	7.00	6.75	6.59	6.45	6.29	6.15	5.97	5.77	5.57
Germany	5.71	5.54	5.51	5.41	5.26	5.14	5.11	5.02	4.95	4.92	4.78	4.57	4.36	4.19	4.13
India	3.48	3.57	3.70	3.84	3.98	3.97	4.11	4.31	4.28	4.38	4.42	4.59	4.69	4.90	5.07
Brazil	3.31	3.39	3.47	3.49	3.43	3.41	3.34	3.24	3.23	3.19	3.20	3.11	3.11	3.07	3.03
Russia	4.94	4.42	3.74	3.46	3.21	3.13	2.89	2.97	3.12	3.20	3.25	3.36	3.41	3.46	3.55
South Africa	0.75	0.74	0.74	0.74	0.74	0.73	0.72	0.71	0.70	0.71	0.71	0.71	0.70	0.70	0.70

Country	2007	2008	2009	2010	2011	2012	2013	2014	2015	2016	2017	2018	2019	2020
United States	18.39	17.81	17.36	16.91	16.51	16.37	16.09	15.95	15.88	15.78	15.63	15.45	15.20	14.92
China	11.40	12.14	13.29	13.96	14.69	15.35	16.02	16.63	17.24	17.71	18.09	18.48	18.91	19.35
Japan	5.39	5.18	4.91	4.88	4.67	4.61	4.53	4.38	4.28	4.18	4.04	3.92	3.81	3.69
Germany	4.05	3.96	3.75	3.71	3.69	3.60	3.51	3.45	3.40	3.33	3.26	3.18	3.10	3.02
India	5.28	5.33	5.80	6.07	6.22	6.34	6.56	6.81	7.09	7.36	7.63	7.91	8.20	8.50
Brazil	3.04	3.10	3.10	3.17	3.16	3.12	3.11	3.01	2.84	2.71	2.67	2.63	2.60	2.56
Russia	3.65	3.73	3.45	3.42	3.43	3.44	3.38	3.29	3.07	2.95	2.87	2.80	2.74	2.68
South Africa	0.70	0.70	0.69	0.68	0.67	0.67	0.66	0.65	0.64	0.63	0.62	0.61	0.60	0.59

* Data from International Monetary Fund, World Economic Outlook Databases, October 2015, www.imf.org/external/pubs/ft/weo/2015/02/weodata/index .aspx, accessed December 2, 2015.

TABLE 6.2. *Share of world GDP at market exchange rates**

Country	1992	1993	1994	1995	1996	1997	1998	1999	2000	2001	2002	2003	2004	2005	2006
United States	26.22	26.80	26.53	24.98	25.69	27.35	29.06	29.82	30.74	31.90	32.00	29.84	28.25	27.84	27.20
China	1.97	2.40	2.04	2.39	2.73	3.04	3.28	3.36	3.60	4.00	4.26	4.28	4.47	4.82	5.36
Japan	15.45	17.20	17.61	17.39	14.92	13.74	12.52	13.63	14.14	12.50	11.60	11.16	10.72	9.72	8.55
Germany	8.54	8.07	8.03	8.46	7.94	7.06	7.18	6.80	5.85	5.86	6.08	6.51	6.50	6.09	5.90
India	1.18	1.11	1.21	1.19	1.27	1.34	1.37	1.44	1.42	1.48	1.53	1.60	1.66	1.77	1.86
Brazil	1.60	1.75	2.03	2.56	2.71	2.82	2.77	1.86	1.96	1.68	1.49	1.45	1.54	1.90	2.17
Russia	0.34	0.72	1.01	1.02	1.24	1.29	0.87	0.60	0.78	0.92	1.01	1.12	1.36	1.62	1.94
South Africa	0.54	0.52	0.51	0.51	0.47	0.48	0.44	0.42	0.41	0.37	0.34	0.45	0.53	0.55	0.53

Country	2007	2008	2009	2010	2011	2012	2013	2014	2015	2016	2017	2018	2019	2020
United States	25.17	23.36	24.16	22.90	21.43	21.90	22.08	22.45	24.44	24.50	24.23	23.99	23.63	23.18
China	6.13	7.23	8.48	9.24	10.35	11.47	12.58	13.40	15.49	16.06	16.32	16.71	17.25	17.78
Japan	7.57	7.70	8.44	8.42	8.16	8.07	5.52	5.96	5.60	5.46	5.38	5.20	5.07	4.93
Germany	5.99	5.98	5.74	5.24	5.19	4.80	4.96	5.01	4.59	4.55	4.45	4.36	4.25	4.16
India	2.15	1.94	2.29	2.61	2.54	2.49	2.48	2.65	2.97	3.12	3.23	3.33	3.46	3.58
Brazil	2.43	2.69	2.79	3.38	3.61	3.27	3.17	3.04	2.45	2.19	2.18	2.17	2.16	2.14
Russia	2.26	2.64	2.05	2.33	2.63	2.73	2.75	2.41	1.68	1.54	1.62	1.69	1.78	1.86
South Africa	0.52	0.46	0.50	0.57	0.58	0.54	0.49	0.45	0.43	0.43	0.42	0.42	0.41	0.41

* Data from International Monetary Fund, World Economic Outlook Databases, October 2015, www.imf.org/external/pubs/ft/weo/2015/02/weodata/index.aspx, accessed December 2, 2015.

If China's annual GDP growth rate continues to outpace that of the United States, it will eventually overtake the United States, but several caveats are in order. First, after three decades of extraordinary double digit growth per year, China's economy has slowed to an announced annual rate of 6.5 percent and Chinese authorities have become concerned as to whether that pace can be sustained. The official growth rate figure is questionable, and significant reductions in China's imports of raw materials suggest that actual economic performance is less than reported. Second, China faces additional problems including limits to its export-led growth model of development, excessive debt levels, and environmental constraints. Third, China will face serious political and social problems. These include issues of legitimacy and governance, but also a demographic crisis as its population and workforce peaks and then begins rapidly shrinking due to the cumulative effects of the one-child policy put in place in 1979–80 and intensified by a gender imbalance that has left the population with more than 33 million fewer women than men.[32]

Another caution is useful in trying to assess the future of China. It is that projections of data can prove inaccurate in surprisingly short spans of time. Such calculations are commonplace in seeking to estimate the size of China's economy in the next five or ten, or even fifteen years. As an example of the forecasting problem, former Treasury Secretary Lawrence Summers provides an American comparison. Estimates of the US federal budget deficit are expressed in projections for the "out" years, but their accuracy is far from certain. The Congressional Budget Office's own evaluations have found that the expected error in its deficit projections just five years out, and not even taking into account unanticipated policy changes, have proved much too pessimistic, amounting to 3.5 percent of GDP in that period.[33] Given the enormous scale of the American economy, this is a *very* large number (a potential error of more than $600 billion over five years) and it serves as a reminder about the difficulty of accurately forecasting vast economic trends.

In addition, thanks to the energy renaissance of recent years, America has become the world's leading producer of oil and natural gas, surpassing both Saudi Arabia and Russia for the first time since 1975.[34] Since the "shale revolution" began in 2009, domestic petroleum production has nearly doubled, oil imports have plunged by nearly half, and the combined total output of petroleum including crude oil, natural gas liquids, and refined products now exceeds that of Saudi Arabia by more than 3 million barrels per day – a complete reversal of the relationship of less than a decade ago.[35] Until the latter part of the

---

[32] Gordon G. Chang, "Shrinking China: A Demographic Crisis," *World Affairs*, May/June 2015, www.worldaffairsjournal.org/print/96727.

[33] Lawrence Summers, "In Showdown Debate, Focus Should be on Growth Instead of Deficit," *Washington Post*, October 13, 2913.

[34] Data from *BP Statistical Review of World Energy 2015*.

[35] According to data from the US Energy Admiration Agency, total US petroleum production in December 2014 averaged 14.83 million barrels per day, compared with 11.52 for Saudi Arabia.

last decade, the country's future seemed to be one in which domestic reserves would be declining more or less inexorably, and greater oil and natural gas imports would be needed. America at that time appeared increasingly vulnerable to the economic and even security effects of a future energy shock. Instead, thanks to technological breakthroughs and cost-effective commercialization of horizontal drilling and fracking, the domestic energy economy has been transformed. Large energy cost advantages for manufacturers based in the United States have stimulated new investment by domestic businesses as well as by others from Europe and Asia. Over the long term, the United States will benefit from abundant domestic energy reserves. In the immediate future, the problem is more one of oversupply of oil and natural gas, though the United States will increasingly become an exporter of liquefied natural gas (LNG).

This energy renaissance provides a major economic benefit, even though the United States is still affected by world oil markets. Over the next decade, America is likely to remain dependent on imports for up to a third of the liquid petroleum consumed within its borders and it can thus be affected by changes in offshore supply and demand. Oil prices are set in a world market, so even if the United States were one day to become a net exporter of oil, a major disruption in the Persian Gulf would be felt here. Nonetheless, America's vulnerability has been enormously lessened and the leverage which major foreign producers of oil and gas such as Russia, Iran, Saudi Arabia, and Venezuela once had has been greatly reduced.

CAN – AND SHOULD – THE UNITED STATES STILL LEAD?

If the United States retains the material capacity to lead, the will to do so is less certain, as are judgments about where and how. Arguments for retrenchment have become increasingly important in both the policy realm and in the academic literature of international relations. Upon taking office, President Obama was often applauded for his call to refocus on "nation-building at home." The American public had become increasingly skeptical about continued troop deployments in Iraq and Afghanistan and more broadly about America's world role. Thus a December 2013 opinion study undertaken by the Pew Research Center for the People and the Press, in collaboration with the Council on Foreign Relations, found 51 percent of the public taking the view that the United States does too much to solve world problems, while just 17 percent saw American involvement as too little.[36] This represented

See Mark J. Perry, "Energy superpower 'Saudi America' has been the world's largest petroleum producer for 26 months in a row," *Carpe Diem* blog, American Enterprise Institute, April 29, 2015, www.aei.org/publication/energy-superpower-saudi-america-has-been-the-worlds-largest-petroleum-producer-for-26-months-in-a-row/?utm_source=paramount&utm_medium=email&utm_content=AEITODAY&utm_campaign=043015.

[36] www.people-press.org/2013/12/03/public-sees-u-s-power-declining-as-support-for-global-engagement-slips/, (accessed January 26, 2016).

the lowest level of support for international engagement since the end of World War II.

Subsequently, with a renewed sense of threat and in reaction to the rise of ISIS and grisly execution videos of Western hostages, the American public has become more supportive. A 2014 national survey by the Chicago Council on Global Affairs found renewed public backing for international engagement and in its 2015 poll, 64 percent of Americans expressed approval for an active US role in world affairs, including the selective use of force.[37]

Foreign policy elites have been more supportive about America continuing to play an actively engaged role in world affairs than the public at large. Indeed, at the same time as the 2013 Pew poll found a majority of Americans describing the United States as doing too much, a companion poll of Council on Foreign Relations respondents (i.e., foreign policy experts and practitioners) gave virtually opposite answers, with just 21 percent saying "too much" and 41 percent "too little."

Public support for an active foreign policy thus cannot be taken for granted. When there is a strong sense of external threat, backing for a robust international role is usually available, but not always. As a case in point, in the years before World War II, President Franklin Roosevelt faced great difficulty in gaining domestic political support to oppose Imperial Japan and Nazi Germany. Even after the outbreak of war on September 1, 1939, antiwar sentiment was so pervasive that the renewal of draft legislation in August 1941 only passed the US House of Representatives by one vote, though the world had been at war for almost two full years and most of Europe and much of East and Southeast Asia had fallen under Nazi and Japanese occupation. The domestic debate was finally transformed with the Japanese attack at Pearl Harbor on December 7, 1941 followed by a massive outpouring of support for the war effort.

Historically, public support for military intervention is often the product of urgent or dramatic events and a rally-round-the-flag effect. Thus in examining public opinion on ten conflicts since the early 1990s, the Gallup organization found public approval at the start of each US military engagement averaging 68 percent.[38] Over a period of time, however, partisan disagreements on

---

[37] Polling took place between May 25 and June 17, 2015 among a national sample of 2034 adults. See Dina Smeltz, Ivo Daalder, Karl Friedhoff, and Craig Kafura, *America Divided: Political Partisanship and U.S. Foreign Policy: Results of the 2015 Council Survey of American Public Opinion and U.S. Foreign Policy*, Chicago Council on Global Affairs, September 2015, p. 2, www.thechicagocouncil .org/sites/default/files/CCGA_PublicSurvey2015.pdf. The Chicago Council's May 2014 poll found 57 percent in favor, though at that time 41 percent wanted the United States to "stay out" of world affairs, the highest figure since the Chicago Council began its surveys in 1974. See Dina Smeltz, Ivo Daalder, and Craig Kafura, *Foreign Policy in the Age of Retrenchment: Results of the 2014 Chicago Council Survey of American Public Opinion and U.S. Foreign Policy*, Chicago: Chicago Council on Global Affairs, 2014, figure 11, page 7, www.thechicagocouncil.org/survey/2014/.

[38] Andrew Dugan, "U.S. Support for Action in Syria is Low Versus Past Conflicts," Gallup.com, September 6, 2013, www.gallup.com/poll/164282/support-syria-action-lower-past-conflicts.aspx.

foreign policy tend to widen, especially when American troops are in combat and the conflict is prolonged. Voters also take their cues from party elites, so that rank-and-file Democrats are more likely to support the foreign policies of a Democrat in the White House, while Republicans are inclined to take cues from a Republican president.[39]

In the case of the Iraq War, partisan disagreements over the Iraq War quickly became intense, even though the principle of armed intervention initially received wide backing. On October 10–11, 2002, the US House of Representatives and the Senate passed resolutions authorizing President George W. Bush to use force in Iraq. The legislation received overwhelming Republican support, and Senate Democrats also voted in favor (29–21). Democratic senators then contemplating the possibility of running for president, among them Hillary Clinton, Joe Biden, John Kerry, and John Edwards voted yes. Unlike their counterparts in the Senate however, a majority of House Democrats opposed the resolution, though nearly 40 percent did vote in favor.

In advance of the Iraq War, public opinion also supported the use of force. Less than a month prior to the March 20, 2003 start of the war, a Gallup Poll found 59 percent in favor and shortly after the start of the conflict, a Pew poll identified 72 percent of the public agreeing with the use of force as the right decision.[40] However, the political consensus did not last. With rising casualties, the failure to find weapons of mass destruction, and no clear end to the conflict in sight, support for the war fell and partisan differences widened dramatically.

The intensely partisan division of opinion became strikingly evident over the following years. For example, at the time of the 2008 presidential nominating conventions, delegates from both parties were asked whether the United States "did the right thing in taking military action against Iraq." Among respondents, the political differences were remarkable. Whereas 80 percent of Republican delegates and 70 percent of Republican voters agreed with the use of force, only 2 percent of Democratic delegates and 14 percent of Democratic voters responded positively.[41] A huge gap was still apparent in 2015, when Republican and Democratic policy leaders were asked whether the war in Iraq had been worth the cost. Though GOP support had declined in comparison with the earlier period, 53 percent still said yes, while just 3 percent of Democratic elites agreed.[42]

---

[39] I elaborate on this point in Robert J. Lieber, "'Politics Stops at the Water's Edge?' Not Recently," in Daniel J. Hopkins and John Sides, eds., *Political Polarization in American Politics* (New York: Bloomsbury, 2015), pp. 61–66.

[40] "Public Attitudes Toward the War in Iraq: 2003–2008," Pew Research Center, March 19, 2008, www.pewresearch.org/2008/03/19/public-attitudes-toward-the-war-in-iraq-20032008/.

[41] *New York Times*, September 1, 2008.

[42] Data from Chicago Council on Global Affairs, Public survey May 2014, Foreign Policy Leaders survey May and July 2014, cited in Joshua Busby, Jonathan Monten, Jordan Tama, Dina Smeltz, Craig Kafura, "Measuring Up: How Elites and the Public See U.S. Foreign Policy," *Foreign Affairs*, June 9, 2015, www.foreignaffairs.com/articles/united-states/2015-06-09/measuring.

Strong differences are evident on other foreign policy issues as well. The Chicago surveys show sharp political elite divisions over increased defense spending and environmental policy. For example, 97 percent of Democratic leaders favor a new international agreement on climate change while just 43 percent of their Republican counterparts agree.[43] On the use of force, a May 2015 public survey, by the Pew Foundation reflects not only a deep split between Democrats and Republicans, but also a more fundamental divide among those who identify as Democrats. To the question, "Should the U.S. use military force to defend a NATO ally against Russia?" 69 percent of Republicans answered yes, but fewer than half of Democrats, just 47 percent agreed.[44] Thus not even a majority of Democrats agreed with a liberal Democratic President Barack Obama in upholding America's commitment to its most important and long-standing alliance of the past seven decades.

This stunning partisan gap between both voters and elites of the two major parties provides vivid evidence of partisan polarization on foreign policy as well as on domestic issues. Differences on the environment, the use of force to support allies, and the war on Iraq also suggest that the steep decline in political moderates is taking place in both parties and not just primarily among Republicans, as some political scientists have argued.[45] Other things being equal, intensified polarization on foreign policy could make it more difficult for any administration to develop a coherent foreign policy based on a leading American role and supported by a domestic consensus.

Despite partisan disagreement between Democratic and Republican policy elites, they do still share some key foreign policy beliefs. According to data from the Chicago Council on Global Affairs, foreign policy leaders agree that the United States remains the most influential country and that strong American leadership is at least somewhat desirable. Elites and the public also agree that the most important foreign policy goals are to prevent the spread of nuclear weapons, secure energy supplies, and combat international terrorism, and majorities even agree in favoring drone strikes, assassinations of terrorist leaders, and air attacks against terrorist training camps and facilities.[46]

For a time, Syria seemed to emerge as an issue but with far less fervor than over Iraq. However, partisan views about the wisdom of force were initially

---

[43] Data from Chicago Council 2014, cited in Busby et al., *ibid.*

[44] Pew Research Center poll, cited in Michael Birnbaum, "NATO Countries Wary of Using Force to Defend against Russia," *Washington Post*, June 10, 2015. The margin of sampling error is 2.8 points.

[45] For example, to the extent these data also reflect the collapse of the moderate-conservative tendency within the Democratic Party, they indicate that political polarization is more symmetrical than a leading expert on American politics, Nolan McCarty, concludes when he writes, "Despite the widespread belief that both parties have moved to the extremes, the movement of the Republican Party to the right accounts for most of the divergence between the two parties." www.washingtonpost.com/blogs/monkey-cage/wp/2014/01/08/what-we-know-and-dont-know -about-our-polarized-politics/.

[46] Data from Chicago Council 2014, cited in Busby *et al., ibid.*

reversed. When in August–September 2013 President Obama briefly appeared to be proposing action in Syria, a majority of Republicans opposed a military strike (58 percent against, 31 percent in favor). Their responses were close to those of the public as a whole (51 percent against, 36 percent in favor), while Democrats remained divided (45 percent in favor, 43 percent opposed).[47] These tepid polling results, and subsequent surveys which showed little support for a use of force beyond the provision of military training advisers and drone attacks, reflected a public weariness with fourteen years of military involvement in the region, the human and material costs of those commitments, and frustration over the inability to win decisively and get out.

With the resurgence of ISIS in 2014 however, Republican elites became more likely to support no-fly zones and arms to insurgents in Syria, though they too remained opposed to sending US troops. In turn, while the formal withdrawal of US forces in December 2011 had temporarily removed Iraq as a major subject of political controversy, the subsequent return of several thousand military trainers and bipartisan concern about ISIS meant that the subject would continue to receive attention. Nonetheless, a majority of voters opposed the reintroduction of American combat troops to Iraq, with only one-third in favor.[48]

Over the past century, support for foreign military intervention has tended to be cyclical. Public support often declines after wars, as was the case following the two world wars, Korea, and Vietnam, and more recently in response to Afghanistan, Iraq, and Libya. However, data from the Gallup organization has shown Afghanistan to be less unpopular than Iraq. According to Gallup, at no point have a majority of Americans expressed the view that the Afghanistan military action was a mistake. Public support for both wars actually has improved with 54 percent saying the Afghanistan War was not a mistake and 46 percent saying the same about Iraq.[49] The rise in support is likely to have been a reaction to the appalling actions of ISIS and continuing American involvement in coalition actions against ISIS, al-Qaeda, and the Taliban.

Despite important areas of agreement, political polarization poses a problem in itself. Congress remains more sharply divided than at any time since the end of reconstruction in the late 1870s.[50] And even the effectiveness of

[47] Gallup poll, September 3–4, 2013, www.gallup.com/poll/164282/support-syria-action-lower-past-conflicts.aspx.

[48] A Rasmussen survey found that only 35 percent favored the dispatch of troops. "Voters Remain Cool to Boots on the Ground in Iraq." Survey of 1,000 likely voters, poll taken May 19–20, 2015, margin of error +/– 3 percentage points. Rasmussenreports.com, May 22, 2015.

[49] Andrew Dugan, "Fewer in U.S. View Iraq, Afghanistan Wars as Mistakes," Gallup.com, June 12, 2015. Margin of sampling error is +/– 3 percentage points. www.gallup.com/poll/183575/fewer-view-iraq-afghanistan-wars-mistakes.aspx?version=print.

[50] Nolan McCarty, Keith T. Poole, and Howard Rosenthal, *Polarized America: The Dance of Ideology and Unequal Riches* (Cambridge, MA: MIT Press, 2006); and "The Polarization of the Congressional Parties," updated January 19, 2014, http://polarizedamerica.com/political_polarization.asp.

governmental institutions and their ability to accomplish needed tasks has become an object of concern.[51] Moreover, the nature and extent of America's international role remains subject to wide debate and disagreement. Thus even those who may agree on the desirability of the United States maintaining an active international presence may nonetheless disagree sharply on specific questions, for example on trade policy, the environment, foreign aid, diplomacy, military assistance, the use of airpower, and whether and when to commit troops to combat in foreign lands.

An impulse to pull back from foreign entanglements has been common after America experiences the intensity and the human costs of warfare. This desire to retrench is not just a matter of cuts in military personnel and the defense budget. The pattern has been one of overreaction and excessive disengagement. As noted earlier in this chapter, the combination of power and diplomacy can be enormously effective when used with prudence and skill and there are numerous foreign policy tools available other than the use of force. Yet the tendency in recent years has been to frame policy choices as requiring either outright conciliation or war. This has resulted in seriously narrowing the practical options available for responding to Russia's invasions of Crimea and Ukraine, Iran's violations of its obligations under the Nuclear Nonproliferation Treaty (NPT), Syria's use of chemical weapons, China's muscle-flexing in East Asia, and the expanding threat posed by ISIS in the Levant.

Foreign policy requires prudent choices and a sense of priorities. Even at the height of its influence, there were always limits to what the United States could achieve and reversals were not uncommon whether in dealing with adversaries or friends. Resources (money, time, political capital, human lives) are never unlimited, and policymakers are ultimately accountable to a domestic audience for the successes and failures of their policies and for the actions they take – or fail to take. In practice, the response to a decade or more of costly intervention in Iraq and Afghanistan has been an overreaction, that is, a retreat, in foreign policy. Some of this pullback has been based on an illusion that conciliation and an outstretched hand to adversaries would produce a benign change in their policies. Another assumption was that retrenchment would neither be harmful to American national interests nor to regional order and security. And a third has been that, in the absence of America's active engagement, others (the "international community", the UN, regional allies) would fill the vacuum without ill effect. Yet in reality, none of these assumptions has proved correct.

Since the end of World War II, the United States has played a unique role in world affairs. Its engagement, in cooperation with others, has been essential

---

[51] Francis Fukuyama emphasizes this point. See "The Ties that Used to Bind: The Decay of American Political Institutions," *The American Interest*, Vol. IX, No. 3, Winter (January/February) 2014, pp. 6–19.

for maintaining a more or less liberal world order, and the consequences of its retrenchment have been detrimental. Moreover, the world does not stand still, and the alternatives to American leadership are mostly those of authoritarian modernization and regional hegemony on the part of countries that do not share the values of liberty, democracy, and the Enlightenment. Putin's Russia in Eastern Europe and the Caucasus, Iran in the Persian Gulf and Mesopotamia, and China in East and Southeast Asia provide cases in point. Many more countries would prefer American predominance to that of Russia, China, or Iran, and any list of allies or friends of the authoritarian powers is a short one. Even so, in the absence of the United States, some will bandwagon with those regimes in the face of power and subtle or not so subtle threats.

Sooner or later, the United States will return to a more robust role. It may do so either because of a reassessment of strategy and policy, or because increasing foreign perils shape the political environment in which decisions are made. In the meantime, America retains the capacity to lead, but until it does so, the world is likely to become a more disorderly and dangerous place, with mounting threats not only to regional stability and economic prosperity, but to the national interests of the United States itself.

Index